T0329042

THE DETERMINATION OF PRODUCTION

To
MY FATHER AND MOTHER

THE DETERMINATION OF PRODUCTION

AN
INTRODUCTION TO THE STUDY OF
ECONOMIZING ACTIVITY

BY

BURGESS CAMERON

CAMBRIDGE
AT THE UNIVERSITY PRESS
1954

CAMBRIDGE
UNIVERSITY PRESS

University Printing House, Cambridge CB2 8BS, United Kingdom

Cambridge University Press is part of the University of Cambridge.

It furthers the University's mission by disseminating knowledge in the pursuit of education, learning and research at the highest international levels of excellence.

www.cambridge.org
Information on this title: www.cambridge.org/9781316509500

First published 1954
First paperback edition 2015

A catalogue record for this publication is available from the British Library

ISBN 978-1-316-50950-0 Paperback

CONTENTS

§1. The aim is to explain how the levels of production (and prices) in society are determined. For this purpose four kinds of data are needed.

§2. A major attribute of productive systems are the opportunities for choice, i.e. for economizing activity.

§3. However, for simplicity we begin with the analysis of a productive system where opportunities for choice are temporarily assumed to be absent.

§4. The institutional data identifying a society comprise: the size, nature and ownership of productive resources including population; the state of technical knowledge; the competitive organization of industry; tastes. These are recorded in four types of functional relation.

§5. With the introduction of two further conditions of equilibrium and of the cost equation, the seven basic relations of the analysis are assembled.

§6. Money is introduced so that absolute (and not merely relative) prices can be determined.

§7. The determination of output and price are analysed in a one-industry system.

§8. The determination of output and price are then analysed in a three-industry system.

§9. The determination of output and price are further analysed in a two-resource system.

§10. Conclusion.

§1. The level of production of the system is set either by the availability of resources or by demand.

§2. The operation of any system is partly determined by its institutions (including its methods of exchange and its traditions).

§1. Definition.

§2. Properties of the function.

§3. Summary.

§4. Specific forms of the function.

§1. The equi-marginal productivity condition determines the choice of ratio in which factors are employed.

§2. An example of substitution.

CONTENTS

*The table is available for download from www.cambridge.org/9781316509500

SYMBOLS

In the interest of brevity, a few standard symbols are used throughout the book instead of the compound nouns they represent. These symbols and their meanings are as follows:

X_i Volume of output of commodity i by the industry producing it (e.g., X_w is the output of wheat, X_f the output of fish in tons).

x_{ai} Volume of input of factor a into the industry producing i (e.g., x_{nw} is the amount of labour (n) employed in the wheat industry).

P_i Price of commodity i per unit of quantity (e.g., P_w is the price of wheat, and P_n the wage-rate or price of labour).

C_i Volume of commodity i demanded by consumers.

M_{TC} Transactions-demand for money required for transactions incident to the production and distribution of consumption goods.

PREFACE

This essay outlines the way in which production and prices are determined in the modern nations of the western world. The book is intended simply to explain how the productive systems of such countries do in fact operate and is in no way concerned to judge whether they ought to be made to operate in some other way. Given the state of technical knowledge attained by a community at any time, the structure and operation of the community's productive system are essentially simple. This simplicity is reflected in the shortness of the essay. The apparent complexity of modern productive systems springs from the mere number of industries and commodities—which is large. But it will be found that by considering hypothetical cases where at most only four or five commodities are produced, we can analyse and understand all the important problems which occur when four or five hundred commodities are produced. Theorems then which are true of, say, a five-industry community will apply equally if the number of industries is greater. Of course the greater the number of industries in the real world, the more difficult is it to apply the theorems, if only because of the volume of arithmetic involved. But this elementary text is concerned only to establish theorems—the task of applying them to real communities cannot be considered here.

Inasmuch as we shall be concerned with the essential characteristics of the system of production, it is inevitable that we should ride roughshod over many points of detail. Thus the picture of the real world here presented may occasionally be a little over-simplified because this is preferable to blurring the really fundamental outlines of the argument. The reader will always be able to insert minor qualifications and additions into the broad framework. What is really important is that he should satisfy himself that the world is in essence as here presented—and this he can only do from his own experience of firm, farm and market-place and by checking the propositions made herein with recorded statistics.

The argument of the essay is cast in the following mould. In the first chapter we analyse a productive system which is very simple, inasmuch as a given quantity of resources is available for employment, all productive factors must be used in fixed proportions, and there is (apart from the technical job of avoiding waste) no opportunity for people to choose between alternative courses of action. It is soon shown that the levels of production of goods are determinate and further that the argument can be readily expanded to deal with any number of industries. Elementary as this first chapter may seem, it provides sufficient theoretical equipment for the reader to follow the extensive researches into the operation of the United States productive system which have been carried out by Professor W. Leontief and his associates and by the U.S. Bureau of Labour Statistics. These undoubtedly comprise the most ambitious economic research programme hitherto undertaken.

Subsequently, however, we analyse economizing activities and from Chapter IV on one opportunity for choice after another is introduced in successive chapters: for example, consumers may buy butter instead of margarine, farmers may employ more or less labour per acre of land, the steelmaster may use a Bessemer converter instead of a Siemens hearth, and so forth. The fact that alternative courses of action do exist gives the individual opportunity to economize, i.e. to make the choice of that alternative which brings him maximum profit or satisfaction. The implications of this maximum postulate are carefully examined so that we may always identify the alternative which will be chosen. When this has been ascertained we can proceed as before to determine the levels of production of the system.

It will be seen then that the essay has two aims: one to provide insight into the manner of working of the productive system; the other to provide a conceptual model which, if we take care in constructing it and can get the correct data, will reproduce the working of the productive systems of our own nations.

In writing this essay I have been grateful for the stimulus of long discussions with many fellows and graduate students in Cambridge. Professors H. W. Arndt and C. F. Carter have read the final manuscript and offered helpful criticisms. My greatest debt is to Professor Carter who persuaded me to try to set down my arguments in simple English. Though the effort has been tremendously instructive (to myself, at least), I am aware that the remaining imperfections are many and for these I am alone responsible.

B.C.

CANBERRA

INTRODUCTION

How the level of production of commodities is determined in society is a problem which may be approached in three ways. The first and perhaps most natural approach is to consider how the overall or aggregate level of output (the 'social product') is determined. The answer to this is illuminating and may be sketched briefly. The elements determining the social product can be considered in two groups. First, if we construct some index measuring the social product,* then, under given conditions of technical knowledge and organization of industry, it is clear that as the level of employment of resources (e.g. of labour)

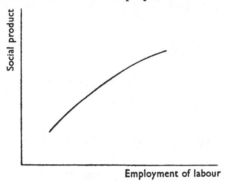

Fig. 1

rises, so also does the volume of the social product. In short the output of the community is directly related to the input of resources engaged in productive activity. This relation may be called the 'aggregate supply function' since it sets out the conditions determining the supply of commodities; it may be expressed diagrammatically (Fig. 1). Second, the demand for commodities is analysed and here the useful distinction is drawn between consumption goods and investment goods. The demand for consumption goods is itself related to the employment of resources, since the higher the level of employment the more commodities will people demand. This relation—called the 'aggregate consumption function'—has also the important characteristic that, in general, if employment rises, consumer-demand will not rise by so much as the resulting increase in output. The reason for this is that, at least after income passes a certain level, people will save a portion of any increase in their incomes. So the curve of the consumption function will at some point

* In particular, if the level of production of all commodities rises and falls in the same proportion, then the meaning of an index of production is quite unambiguous.

xi

fall away below the aggregate supply function as in Fig. 2. Now the demand for investment goods (machines, factory buildings) fluctuates from year to year because a firm makes heavy investment demands while building a factory and its demand then drops sharply until equipment begins to wear out. If we can ascertain the level of investment demand for any year (for example by circulating a questionnaire among firms) then we know the aggregate

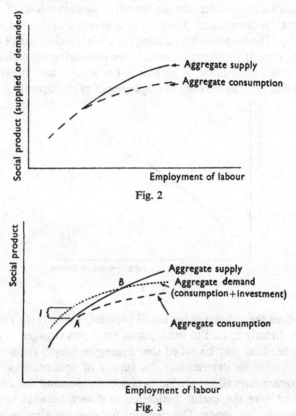

Fig. 2

Fig. 3

demand function since this is the sum of consumption and investment demands and may be represented as in Fig. 3. The intersection of the aggregate demand and aggregate supply schedules (point B in Fig. 3) gives us the equilibrium level of the social product (and of employment). For if production is above this level, unsold stocks of goods will accumulate on the manufacturers' shelves, and if it is below this level, manufacturers will run down their stocks.

Perhaps the most illuminating aspect of the above analysis is its usefulness in explaining changes in the level of production. Suppose for example that investment demand in Fig. 3 is zero; then the equilibrium level of production is given at *A*. If now investment demand rises from zero to *I* then the social product rises to the level of *B*. It will be observed that the level of production has risen by much more than the increase required to satisfy investment demand. The reason for this (the so-called 'multiplier effect') is that the increase in employment of workers in the investment-goods industries results in an increase in expenditure by them on consumer-goods so that employment in consumer-goods industries rises. These workers also spend more on consumer-goods and so employment rises again in the consumer-goods trades. The process tapers off, however, as at each round of employment some income is saved and finally production and employment reach the position *B*. It can be readily shown, for example, that if people save a quarter of any increase in their income, then the total rise in production from *A* to *B* will be four times the increase in investment demand.

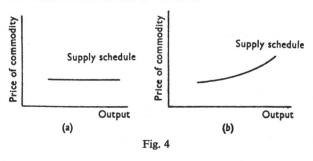

Fig. 4

The foregoing analysis of the aggregate level of production is capable of considerable refinement.* But it is fundamentally deficient in that it tells us nothing about the level of production of individual industries. This brings us to consider the second approach, which analyses the determination of output of the individual industry as follows: once again the elements determining output are divided into two groups.† First, with given technical knowledge and organization of industry, then, if we also know the prices of all factors used, we can draw up a supply schedule showing how much the industry will produce at each price. The supply schedule, for example, may be horizontal if the industry can expand output at constant efficiency, or rising if expanded production involves diminishing returns to scale (Fig. 4). Second, if consumers' tastes are unchanging, then, if we know the incomes of all individuals and the prices of all other goods, we can draw up a demand schedule showing how much of this industry's commodity will be demanded at each possible price—it being fairly clear that customarily people will demand more, the lower the price (Fig. 5). Bringing the supply and demand schedules together we find the equilibrium level of output and price of the

* For example, see Chapter II.
† For simplicity let us consider a consumer-good industry.

industry's product determined by their intersection (Fig. 6), for if price were greater than this equilibrium level the supply would exceed the demand so that stocks would accumulate (and conversely).

The foregoing analysis is also capable of showing us the 'first effects' of institutional change, i.e. of changes in the demand or supply conditions in the industry. For example, if tastes change such that there is a greater preference for milk then the demand schedule for milk lifts upwards from DD to $D'D'$; the first effect of this, if the dairy industry is producing under conditions of

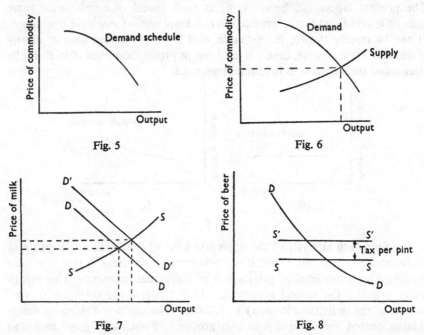

Fig. 5   Fig. 6

Fig. 7   Fig. 8

rising cost, will be a rise in both the price and the output of milk as in Fig. 7. Or if the Government imposes a higher excise tax on beer, thus lifting the supply schedule throughout by the amount of the tax, the first effect will be a fall in production and a rise in price (Fig. 8).

However, this 'partial equilibrium' analysis (as it is called) of the determination of industrial output is deficient in two respects. First, it is severely limited by the need to assume that all factor-prices, all other commodity prices and the total level of incomes are known—whereas these are variables which it is the aim of any comprehensive analysis to determine. Second, in examining the effects of institutional change the analysis assumes all these other prices and incomes to be constant. This is all very well for the examination of first effects, but it means that second effects are ignored. For example, a higher beer price will cause people to turn to other beverages whose prices in turn may thus be forced to rise and this in turn maintains the demand for beer at a higher level than was the case when all other prices were assumed constant—in short, secondary effects through price substitution have been ignored; further, if the beer industry is of any size then a fall in its output involves a fall in factor incomes and hence a fall in demand for beer, which the analysis also ignores. Partial equilibrium analysis then is useful in indicating the nature and size of first effects, but (and especially if the industry is large) second effects may also be large, and so partial equilibrium analysis may give us no accurate indication of the final results of institutional change.

These defects can be overcome only by simultaneously analysing the determination of production in each industry in the entire productive system. This is accomplished by the third approach (called 'general equilibrium' analysis) which is the subject of this essay. This approach performs the functions of each of the first two, but is without their defects. Indeed, it can be formally shown that both aggregative and partial analysis are each limited aspects of the vastly more powerful general equilibrium analysis.

CHAPTER I

THE SYSTEM OF PRODUCTION
(FIRST MODEL)

§ 1. This essay aims to explain how the level of production of commodities is determined in society. The argument proceeds from a simple case in this chapter and is later developed to deal with a complex society such as our own.

Given that the ownership of natural resources has been allocated among the community, the further information we need about a society falls under four heads: Resources;   Technical knowledge; Organization of industry; Tastes.

The meaning of these four categories may be briefly elaborated.

The inventory of all productive resources includes the population (both as regards its size and age-distribution), mineral resources, the configuration and chemical composition of the earth, climate and the nature and extent of fauna and flora. It includes too the heritage of produced resources such as buildings, dams and bridges. All these data are assumed unchanging save in so far as our analysis of the processes of production will show them to be changed. Along with the distribution of ownership of factors we assume the existence of an entrepreneur class and of the firms which they manage and direct. The emergence of certain individuals as entrepreneurs is to be explained both by the possession of certain psychological qualities and personal aptitudes and perhaps to a lesser extent by the ownership of resources. That production is carried on in firms rather than households is explained by the resulting greater opportunities for specialization and so greater production.

As regards the remaining three categories of data: The state of technical knowledge and ability is assumed to be given, as also is the entire range of persons' psychological tastes. The nature of monopoly elements, if such exist, in the organization of industry is also known. Finally, it is assumed that events—such as geological change—do not occur which are 'external' in the sense that they are not necessary to the operation of the productive system.

The reason why we need data of just these four kinds is not far to seek: The 'system of production' of a community is based on its collection of natural resources (including labour), and, by virtue of the technical knowledge of engineers, farmers and the like, these resources are co-ordinated in firms and farms to produce consumer-goods. However, the aggregate output of a commodity depends too on the 'organization of the industry', since, for example, the firms producing that commodity may be able to restrict the entry of other

1

firms into the industry, and by so restricting output are able to obtain a greater rate of profit. If the above three kinds of data indicate the 'potential productivity' of the system, the tastes of the individuals determine what is in fact produced—both the total level of production and the relative outputs of the several kinds of commodity. On the one hand, the tastes of individuals (in their role of owners of resources) determine how much of those resources will be rented for use in producing goods (for there is virtue in leisure and no less in virgin parkland). On the other hand, having received incomes by virtue of their ownership of factors, the pattern of expenditures of individuals (in their role of consumers) then determines the relative level of output of each kind of consumer-good.

§2. Before proceeding to examine these four categories in more detail, attention should be directed to a most important attribute of productive systems: the opportunities for choice.

Experience shows that there are insufficient resources available to satisfy the material wants of all members of society, who, because of this, seek to 'economize'—to obtain greater and ultimately maximum satisfaction from those resources. Opportunities for economizing decisions may be open to the individual in his role of owner of resources, of businessman or of consumer—and any such decision affects the levels of production. These opportunities for economy may be listed:

(1) Choice between use or non-use of resources in the current period, e.g. between leisure and exertion.

(2) Choice of the date of final use of the services of resources. It is also convenient to divide these into:

(i) resources exhausted by use, e.g. mineral deposits;

(ii) resources not exhausted by use, e.g. current labour exertion, whose results may be used now to produce consumption goods or may be stored in the form of personal skills and knowledge or embodied in material equipment and stocks.

(3) Choice of the composition of production for current consumption, e.g. between beer and cheese; and likewise as to the composition of production for future needs. (Such choice depends upon the non-specificity of factors.)

(4) Choice between methods of production, e.g. between a handicraft and machine process.

(5) Choice between factors in the productive process. Apart from 'getting the most out of' a given resource in a given use (i.e. what we call 'technical efficiency'), opportunity to economize in the actual production of a commodity depends on the existence of substitutability between factors.*

(6) Choice between locations of production.

* In this essay the term 'factor' is used generically to apply to all kinds of input whether produced or non-produced.

2

(7) Choice of the quantity of factors to use in any plant—i.e. the problem of effective allocation of factors as between plants making the same commodity.

(8) Choice as regards 'hedging', e.g. by diversifying one's products, by selling in a larger number of markets, or by paying fire or marine insurance premiums.

(9) Innovation—or generally the use of initiative in productive enterprise. This includes the productive application of any invention or of any new knowledge.

In résumé, to determine the current levels of production, maximizing decisions to be made are: whether to use resources currently; if so, when finally to use their services; what commodities to produce; by what method to produce them; and with what combination (ratio) of factors; where to produce; and how many factors to use in any one plant. In addition, individuals and firms must decide whether to hedge; and finally there is the possibility of innovation.

§3. This analysis is designed from the outset to examine the operation of the entire system of production. It is clearly convenient, therefore, that much of the detail which characterizes any real productive system should be temporarily ignored in order that the overall operation of the system may be more readily grasped. There is, indeed, one step we can most appropriately take at this point which will prevent excessive complexity obscuring the conception of the entire system. We shall assume certain facts to be true of society, the effect of which is to eliminate (until later chapters) the several opportunities for choice. Broadly, it is assumed that the decision has previously been made as to the quantity of resources to be used in productive activity and, assuming there is no further room for choice, the operation of the system is examined. Stating the case in more detail, the following nine assumptions are required: The society is one in which institutional considerations (and perhaps human inertia) have determined the statutory length of the working week, while we also know tastes to be such that all factors of production are available for employment and at any price they can command; in which the level of inventories is fixed, there are no investment goods, and the amount of current exertion to be stored in the form of personal skills and knowledge is predetermined by the educational system; in which there is but a single commodity (for example, fish or wheat); and but one method of producing that commodity; in which there is but one variable scarce resource, labour; in which the location of productive activity is predetermined (say by the site of fishing banks); in which the industry is controlled by a single board of directors;* and in which there is neither opportunity for hedging; nor is innovation permitted.

---

* This assumption of a single firm is far stronger than we need and is made for brevity only. As will be discussed later, the less restrictive assumption only is here needed, that: for any given group of available resources used, the aggregate output obtainable from them is the same, irrespective of the number of firms into which the industry is divided.

3

We find ourselves, then, viewing a simple society of, shall we say, fishermen. In the circumstances outlined there is clearly no opportunity for saving, and the entire income of individuals will be devoted to current consumption. Simple as is the situation, it contains the seeds of the entire conception of a more complex modern society—towards which we shall rapidly progress after this elementary analysis has been completed—in which opportunities exist for economizing activity.

§4. The four kinds of data which identify our society may be restated in the form of functional relations. Thus, from a knowledge of existing resources and of the tastes of the owners of those resources we may record the *factor-supply function*, which shows, say, in the case of labour, the number of hours per week a man is willing to work at various hourly wage-rates. It may be

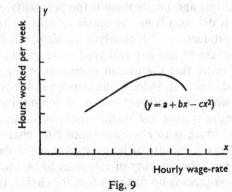

Fig. 9

found, for example, that the function has the shape given in Fig. 9—this shape suggesting that, although at first a higher wage-rate induces more work, after his income reaches a certain level, leisure becomes of increasing relative value to the worker and his hours worked decline. Whatever the shape of the curve, it is clear that the function can be recorded most briefly by simply writing down the formula for the curve over the range indicated, $y = a + bx - cx^2$.

The reason for recording data in the form of functional relations is that, as will soon become clear, the levels of output are in fact determined by the set of these relations and it is only by recording in this way that we can rapidly compute what the equilibrium levels of output and price will be. The next function we need is the *production function*, which states the relation between the rates of input of productive factors and the rate of output of commodities, such that, given the state of technical knowledge and any technically fixed inputs, the function expresses the maximum product obtainable from any combination of variable factors. The production function has the merit of recording with exceptional brevity the state of technical knowledge and ability. The function is explicitly drawn up with respect to a plant,

4

a firm or an industry. For example, the production function of the fishing industry might be drawn as in Fig. 10, or stated yet more briefly by simply writing down the formula for the curve, $y = 2x - 0\cdot05x^2$.

The *entry function* expresses the number of firms in the industry as a function of the rate of profit on output.* Practical experience suggests that this entry function is frequently of the simple form of a 'normal profit condition', i.e. a rate of profit has been established as normal to the industry, and the entry of firms is determined by this prevailing rate,† e.g. normal rate = 7 % (value of output).

It is not difficult to see how the entry function or normal profit condition records the degree of the competitive organization of industry. A particular profit rate may be normal to an industry for two characteristically different reasons. First, where no firm in the industry has any appreciable control over

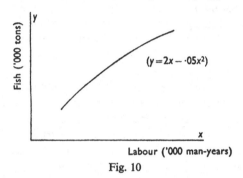

Labour ('000 man-years)

Fig. 10

total supply of the commodity, no firm will be able to obtain a profit greater than the minimum it demands, for any attempt to obtain a greater rate will be defeated by the action of competitors. Under such organization of industry, the minimum or 'normal' rate will be established. Secondly, for a variety of reasons—patent rights, secret processes, threat of trade war, the size of capital investment required—firms in the industry may have control over the total supply of the commodity in that they can prevent or obstruct the entry of new firms. The essence of a monopoly position lies in control of price, and this derives from control of total supply, which in turn must depend upon conditions of entry. Firms possessing such a monopoly position may determine (tacitly or by agreement) the 'normal' rate of profit in the industry.

* Alternatively we may say: the number of firms is a function of the ratio of the price of the output to the sum of the weighted prices of non-entrepreneurial inputs, the weights being the respective equilibrium input coefficients (i.e. ratio of input to output).

† The normal profit condition stands in the same relation to the general entry function that a perfectly elastic supply curve bears to an upward sloping supply curve. We speak of a normal profit 'condition' because it is a condition of equilibrium that the normal rate should prevail.

Even if a new firm enters the industry, both it and the old firms may prefer to maintain the old profit rate rather than begin a price war. Like all institutional data, of course, the industry's 'normal' profit rate is subject to revision, but for the present we shall assume it to be fixed.

The notion that the entrepreneur has a definite conception of a 'normal' or equilibrium profit—such that he will always seek to produce a commodity yielding a profit not less than this—is a familiar one, and has two variants: it may be an absolute figure or a rate, especially a rate on output.* The first variant derives from the view that the entrepreneur has definite 'transfer-earnings'—the highest reward for his effort he could receive in some other occupation and failing the receipt of which he will transfer to that occupation. (In fact, of course, the cost of such transfer must be taken into account, as also such job-attractions as prestige, while a further major element is the additional reward demanded for managing riskier enterprises.) The second derives from the view that a normal rate gives a greater absolute return if the entrepreneur's efforts succeed in expanding sales and hence gives him an incentive, as well as from the view that the use of a rate facilitates his accounting procedures. These two views are not irreconcilable. Here the notion of a profit rate is used—taking the view that the entrepreneur's evaluation of his transfer-earnings is a major determinant of the magnitude of the rate.

The *consumption function* for a particular commodity (say butter) states that the quantity of the commodity purchased is determined by the income of individuals, by the price of the commodity and by the prices of other (competing and complementary) commodities. We could say that the function expresses the individuals' tastes (or portion of them) in behaviourist form— by which is meant that, knowing individuals' incomes and the ruling market prices, we know how they will behave in the market, i.e. how much they buy.

A complete consumption function cannot be satisfactorily drawn on a two-dimensional diagram because the larger number of variables requires more dimensions. However, it can readily be recorded in algebraic form, e.g.

$$C_i = a + bY + cP_i + dP_j,$$

where C_i is quantity demanded of commodity i;

P_i is the price of i;

P_j is the price of j, another commodity or commodity-group;

and Y is the income of individuals;

a, b, c, d being constants, and c probably being negative, so that, when price rises, quantity demanded falls.

---

* Or on capital. The unsophisticated view that the rate is on output is here taken largely because of the nature of the available statistical data against which these arguments may be tested.

The function may, of course, be of some other form; for example, one form which has been extensively tested by investigators is that where the function is linear in natural logarithms $(C_i = a.Y^b.P_i^c.P_j^d)$. The exact form of the function need not detain us here, however, but will be discussed in a later chapter.

§5. The argument developed so far may now be summarized and extended. The institutional data of a society are first recorded in three functions:

> The factor-supply function;
> The production function;
> The consumption function.

What level of output will be produced cannot be known, however, until we introduce conditions which the equilibrium level of output must satisfy. There are three of these conditions:

> The normal profit condition;
> The necessary maximum condition;
> The intersector condition.

The first of these (normal profit) records the remainder of the institutional data. The second is the condition that if there are alternative courses of action, the individual or firm will follow that course which yields maximum personal satisfaction or profit. Discussion of the maximum condition may be postponed because we have temporarily eliminated all alternative courses (by the assumptions in §3). The third (intersector) condition is that the quantity produced of a commodity shall equal the sum of all demands for it from other sectors (or industries). In other words, if the steel industry finds that its stocks of steel for sale are either rising or falling, then it is not in equilibrium.

Finally, we must introduce the businessman's profit and loss account because this states explicitly that the value of production equals the sum of all costs. So we have the seventh relation:

> The cost equation

or profit and loss account, showing the distribution of the value of output between all costs.

The first stage of the inquiry has been completed with the assembly of these seven relations. Subject to slight modifications introduced later, it is true to say that they comprehend all our information about the system of production and from them all our deductions regarding the system are made. It may further be emphasized that even in the later more complicated models the productive system will still be found to be completely described in terms of these seven basic relations. The sole qualifications to this statement are the additional relations required to demonstrate the determination of money prices and the interest rate; and the study of interregional trade involves the further introduction of one familiar equilibrium condition.* These apart, the productive system is formally assembled by setting down for *each* industry the following relations:

The production function;
The necessary maximum condition;
The normal profit condition;
The intersector condition;
The cost equation.

This 'industry five-set' is the primary building block with which we erect the structure of production. In addition, a factor-supply function indicates the availability of each original resource as *input* for productive activity in these industries; and at the other end of the structure a consumer-demand function is needed to determine the *output* of each final commodity.

§6. From the relations set out above we shall determine the level of production in a society. As yet, we cannot determine the level of money prices, although the data are sufficient to determine the *relative* prices of goods. Since, however, our own society employs money it is convenient to introduce it into our analysis at the outset. Having done this, we shall proceed directly in the next section to show how the model (or system of relations) may be applied.

Accordingly we now recognize the existence of a transactions demand for money: individuals seek a commodity which is widely acceptable in the settlement of contractual obligations, for its use renders more efficient the process of exchange and also, by creating increased opportunity for specialization, stimulates production. Comparative stability in value is the major quality, possessing which a commodity will be widely accepted and so come to be used as a medium of exchange in the everyday transactions involved in producing and distributing the social product. We shall call it the money-commodity, or briefly 'money'.† Assuming for the present, then, that the sole demand for money is to satisfy the transactions motive, we now introduce both money and the banks which manufacture it.‡

The quantity of money required to finance the production and distribution of the social product varies only with the physical volume of production, the prices of commodities, the degree of vertical integration of industry and the

---

* That the price of a commodity shall vary between regions by an amount equal to its costs-of-transfer between those regions.

† We are temporarily postponing introduction of the fact that people also have solid reasons for wanting a 'unit of account' (the essential prerequisite again being anticipated approximate stability in exchange value). For, if the same commodity comes to serve both functions, as is usually the case, it may also be used as a store of value—a fact whose implications will be introduced in Chapter VII (see especially §4).

‡ We assume that the quantity of money is determined by the banks. We shall here discuss neither the manner in which the commercial banks perform this function nor the ways in which the central bank may control them. See R. S. Sayers, *Modern Banking*.

payments habits* of individuals and firms. Assuming the last two determinants to be invariant over long periods of time, we conclude that the transactions demand for money is functionally related to the value of the social product $[M_{TC} = \phi(P_i X_i)]$, the simplest possibility being that, when the value of the social product doubles, so also does the transactions demand, i.e.

$$M_{TC} = k.P_i.X_i,$$

where k is a fixed coefficient.†

However, as regards the form of this relation, it must be noted that the transactions motive results not only in a demand for funds to purchase current inputs, but also in a demand for the purchase of *existing* capital assets. Since it is not obvious that there should be a simple relation between this latter demand for active balances and the value of current production, the money equation may well not be of the simple fixed-coefficient form. The form of the function then is a matter for empirical investigation.‡ Knowing it, and knowing also the supply of money, we are able to determine not merely the relative prices of commodities and factors, but also their absolute prices in terms of money. For example, if there were but a single commodity, fish, and the transactions demand for money were of the simple form

$$M_{TC} = k.P_f.X_f,$$

then, knowing that M_{TC} must equal the given supply of money and having determined the level of output X_f, the money price of fish P_f can be immediately deduced. It is clear in these circumstances that the greater the supply of money the greater will the absolute price level have to be.§

§ 7. Consider now a simple system of production as described by the assumptions of §3 above. We wish to ascertain the equilibrium level of output

---

* The two important considerations are: the *period* between the individual's settling days; the extent to which the *dating* of these periods is the same for different individuals (and firms).

† If the transactions demand function were of this simple form, then, with a little heroic abstraction, we may restate it as follows:

$$M_{TC} = \left(\frac{t+1}{V}\right).P_i.X_i,$$

a form of the so-called 'quantity theory'.

Key: t is the degree of integration of industry as measured by the number of firms through which, on the average, the total final value of output must pass in the vertical process of production and distribution. (The addition of unity is for factor-remuneration.) V is the transactions velocity of circulation of money.

‡ See J. W. Angell, *The Behaviour of Money*.

§ In visualizing the role of money in the productive system it is simplest to conceive of a given money supply being created by the banks and advanced to manufacturers who pay one another for materials and pay wages and rents to the owners of primary factors. These last use their money receipts to purchase consumer-goods from the factories and at the end of the period the entrepreneurs are able to repay the banks—the money having completed its circular flow. The historical creation of the money supply, of course, is a far more haphazard process but, once created, its function is the same.

of the system. While so doing, the equilibrium prices of both factors (in this case, labour) and commodities will also be determined. The following example illustrates the method of analysis:

The community examined has a labour force of 10,000 men. The sole productive activity is fishing and the production function of the industry is

$$X_f = 2x_{nf} - 0.05x_{nf}^2,$$

where x_{nf} is the input of labour in thousand man-years, X_f is the output of fish in thousand tons. The normal profit rate for the industry is 6 % of the value of output. Finally, the sole demand for money being for the carrying out of transactions in the market, this demand is given by

$$M_T = 0.07X_f . P_f,$$

where M_T is the transactions demand for money and P_f is the price of fish; the supply of money from the banking system is £0·5 million.

From this information the level of output is immediately derived. Since consumers spend their entire income, the limit to production is here set only by the physical scarcity of labour. The entire labour force will thus be employed and will produce 15,000 tons of fish. From the financial information, it follows that the price of fish will be £476·2 per ton. By drawing up the industry's profit and loss account we also find that the wage of labour is £671·4 per annum. These results are summarized in Table 2.

Table 2. *Transactions during twelvemonth*

Output of	Price (£)	Sold to (£m.)	
		1	Consumers
1. Fishing (ton)	476		7·14
2. Labour (men)	671	6·71	—
3. Profit	—	0·43	—
Value produced	—	7·14	—

§8. Having considered the simple case of a single industry, the analysis may now be extended to a society having any number of industries. To illustrate the development of the argument consider a three-industry system: there is now a timber industry in addition to the fishing industry and part of the output of each is absorbed by a smoked-fish industry. For simplicity we shall suppose that each industry is of constant scale efficiency, i.e. if the industry doubles (or halves) its input of factors of production then its output also doubles (or halves). This assumption can be dropped whenever convenient. It is also to be assumed that consumers allocate an unchanging

10

proportion of their income to each of the three consumer-goods—for as yet we do not wish to admit opportunity for consumers to make economizing decisions in choosing between goods.

It will be observed that, as labour is for the present the sole variable scarce factor, there is for any level of output a *technically* most efficient routine of producing a commodity,* viz. that which uses least labour directly and indirectly. Since further we assume here that each industry is of constant scale efficiency, this routine of production will be identical for all levels of output. Hence the production function will be of the simple fixed-coefficient form where each input is used in fixed proportion to the level of output. This form of the production function is accordingly used below.

For brevity we may also in the following example omit the strictly monetary data. The effect of this is that we can determine (in addition to the levels of output) only *relative* prices of commodities and factors. For example, if we were to take the wage-rate as unity (or 'numéraire'), then all other prices may be expressed as so many 'wage-units'. The introduction of the monetary data, as in §7, would enable us to determine the wage-rate in £ and hence to know the money prices of all other commodities.

The data for the three-industry system may then be set down:

Factor supply function

The labour force of 10,000 men available at any price they can obtain.

Production functions

Fishing. The intake of labour is 0·6 man-year per ton of output.
Smoked-fish. The intake of labour is 0·08 man-year per ton of output.
   The intake of timber is 3·5 tons per ton of output.
   The intake of fish is 1·8 tons per ton of output.
Timber. The intake of labour is 0·01 man-year per ton of output.

Normal profit

The profit rate in each industry is 6 % of the value of output.

Consumption functions

Consumers spend 0·6 of their income on fresh fish, 0·3 on smoked-fish and 0·1 on timber for household fuel.

To these data we may add for each industry:

	Its intersector condition;
and	Its cost equation.

---

* This is never true where more than one input is involved. Strictly speaking, entre-preneurship is also an input here, but we shall avoid this difficulty for purposes of exposition by assuming the same profit rate throughout all industry.

We may now proceed to determine the equilibrium levels of output through the following steps:

First, consider the labour requirements of all industries. The labour requirements of the fishing industry are 0·6 man-year per ton, and so for a final demand for fish of C_f are $0·6C_f$. The labour requirements of the smoked-fish industry are: directly 0·08 man-year per ton; indirectly through the input of timber, 0·01 of 3·5 man-years per ton; indirectly through the input of fish, 0·6 of 1·8 man-years per ton. Hence the total labour requirement of the smoked-fish industry for a final demand for smoked-fish of C_s is $1·195C_s$. Finally, the labour requirement of the timber industry for a final demand of C_t is $0·01C_t$. Hence the total labour requirement of all industry is

$$(0·6\,C_f + 1·195\,C_s + 0·01\,C_t)\ \text{man-years},$$

and this must equal 10,000, since we know that the entire labour force will be employed—the scarcity of labour being the sole limit to production. So we have

$$0·6\,C_f + 1·195\,C_s + 0·01\,C_t = 10,000, \tag{1}$$

this being the overall requirement which limits *aggregate* consumption of all commodities by the available labour force.

Secondly, however, we know from the consumption function that the value of fresh fish consumed is six times the value of timber consumed and twice the value of smoked-fish consumed. We may write it

$$C_f P_f = 6 C_t P_t, \tag{2}$$

and

$$C_f P_f = 2 C_s P_s, \tag{3}$$

these being the requirements determining the *relative* rates of consumption of the several commodities. Together, these three equations can tell us the consumption and so the output of each commodity. But first the prices of the commodities must be ascertained, since, in this example, it is the *values* of the commodities consumed that are in fixed proportions.

Thirdly, then, relative prices must be known, and this, in the present circumstances of a single scarce resource, is readily determined since the exchange value of a good is determined by its labour content (or 'embodied labour'). Proceeding to solve for prices then, the cost equations of the three industries may be written down

$$\begin{cases} 0·94 X_f P_f = x_{nf} P_n, \\ 0·94 X_s P_s = x_{ns} P_n + x_{ts} P_t + x_{fs} P_f, \\ 0·94 X_t P_t = x_{nt} P_n, \end{cases}$$

and if we use the production function data (e.g. $x_{nf} = 0·6 X_f$) we can substitute for the input flows (e.g. x_{nf}) to obtain

$$\begin{cases} 0·94 P_f = 0·6 P_n, \\ 0·94 P_s = 0·08 P_n + 3·5 P_t + 1·8 P_f, \\ 0·94 P_t = 0·01 P_n, \end{cases}$$

12

from which, if we take the wage-rate to be unity ($P_n = 1$), we immediately read off the prices expressed in wage-units: the price of (fresh) fish is 0·638 wage-units per ton, the price of smoked-fish is 1·346 wage-units per ton and the price of timber is 0·0106 wage-units per ton.*

Finally, returning to equations (1), (2) and (3) we ascertain the levels of consumption to be 11,196 tons of (fresh) fish, 2653 tons of smoked-fish and 112,170 tons of timber, and from these the levels of output can be computed. These results are conveniently set out in Table 3.

Table 3. *Transactions during twelvemonth*

Output of	Price (wage-unit)	Sold to (wage-unit)			
		1	2	3	Consumers
1. Fishing (ton)	0·638	—	3,050	—	7,139
2. Smoked-fish (ton)	1·346	—	—	—	3,570
3. Timber (ton)	0·0106	—	98	—	1,189
4. Labour (man-year)	1·0	9,583	212	1,215	—
5. Profit	—	606	210	72	—
Value produced	—	10,189	422	1,287	—

§9. Let us now increase the realism of the argument by introducing a second scarce resource, namely, land of given quality. By assuming that all inputs into an industry are used in fixed proportions, all economizing opportunities are still excluded (since the businessman cannot substitute one input for another). For simplicity we assume a constant level of efficiency in each industry.

Consider then a simple society where the sole industries are wheat and fish production.† The community is specified as follows:

Factor supply function

The labour force of 10,000 men and also the territory of 400,000 acres (of equal fertility) are available at any price they can obtain.

Production functions

Fishing. The intake of labour is 0·6 man-year per ton of output.
Wheat. The intake of labour is 0·1 man-year per ton of output.
    The intake of land is 6·0 acres per ton of output.

---

* The price of a commodity (expressed in wage-units) here equals the number of man-hours required to produce it, 'grossed up' by the profit margin.
† Any number of industries can be handled equally well.

Normal profit

The profit rate in each industry is 6 % of the value of output.

Consumption functions

Consumers spend 0·7 of their income on wheat and 0·3 on fish.

The introduction of a second original resource involves a variation in the procedure for ascertaining the equilibrium levels of output for we must decide which resource will ultimately limit production. Now, of labour, we know the following to be true in the present example: output rises when more labour is employed (at least in fishing); labour is willing to work for any wage; labour can work in an industry where land usage* is zero (while the reverse is not true). Hence we may take it that, as output is not limited by consumer-demand, the entire labour force will be employed. Of land, we know that it will either all be employed or its price will be zero. It is necessary to ascertain which of these is the case. If we begin by assuming the price of land (P_l) to be zero, then if the figure obtained for land usage exceeds 400,000 acres, we know that we are incorrect and that the correct price can then be found by reworking the argument on the basis that land usage is 400,000 acres. We may now proceed to solve the problem following the procedure of §8.†

As before, then, the reader will find that the overall requirement limiting aggregate consumption is

$$0 \cdot 6 C_f + 0 \cdot 1 C_w = 10,000, \tag{i}$$

while the requirement determining the relative rates of consumption of the two commodities is

$$3 C_w P_w = 7 C_f P_f. \tag{ii}$$

First solving for prices ($P_l = 0$ by assumption), we find that the price of fish is 0·638 wage-units and that of wheat 0·106 wage-units. Inserting this information in (i) and (ii), we have the result that $C_f = 4990$ tons and $C_w = 70,060$ tons. But this latter output of wheat would require an acreage of 420,360. As the society cannot meet this requirement it is clear that a positive price will be set on land. Accordingly we must now rework our argument using the knowledge that the price of land will be positive and that all land available (viz. 400,000 acres) will be employed.

There are now therefore two overall requirements limiting aggregate consumption by the available land and labour, viz.

$$0 \cdot 6 C_f + 0 \cdot 1 C_w = 10,000, \tag{1}$$
$$6 C_w = 400,000, \tag{2}$$

from which we deduce that $C_w = 66,666 \cdot 6$ tons and $C_f = 5555 \cdot 5$ tons, these being also the figures of total output.

* Both directly and indirectly through materials.

† In a community where both land and labour are employed in each industry, either land or labour may set the ultimate limit to productive activity. The solution can then only be found by patiently exploring each alternative.

14

Prices may now be determined from the remaining information—relative prices being no longer determined only by labour-content but also by relative demand for the commodities containing more or less land-services:

$$3C_wP_w = 7C_fP_f,\tag{3}$$

$$0\cdot94P_f = 0\cdot6P_n,\tag{4}$$

$$0\cdot94P_w = 0\cdot1P_n + 6P_l,\tag{5}$$

from which we ascertain the price of fish to be 0·638 wage-units, that of wheat 0·124 wage-units, while that of land is 0·0027 wage-units.* These results are summarized in Table 4.

Table 4. *Transactions during twelvemonth*

Output of	Price (wage-unit)	Sold to (wage-unit)		
		1	2	Consumers
1. Fishing (ton)	0·638	—	—	3,540
2. Wheat (ton)	0·124	—	—	8,270
3. Labour (man-year)	1·0	3,333	6,667	—
4. Land (acre)	0·0027	—	1,100	—
5. Profit	—	207	503	—
Value produced	—	3,540	8,270	—

§10. In this chapter we have given precise meaning to the concept of 'a system of production' as an entity absorbing natural resources and manufacturing them into commodities demanded by consumers. Any productive system is adequately specified by the seven types of relation discussed in §§4 and 5, and from these the equilibrium rates of output may be ascertained. It is true that so far our model of the system of production is free from many complications of real life, but these complications (for all their importance)

* For example, $P_w = \dfrac{7}{3}\cdot\dfrac{C_f}{C_w}\cdot P_f$ wage-units, and by substitution we find from this that

$$P_w = \frac{7}{3}\cdot\frac{6}{0\cdot94}\cdot\left\{\frac{1}{40} - \frac{1}{60}\right\} \text{ wage-units,}$$

where

(a) 7/3 is the ratio of the value of wheat to fish demanded (the 'strength of demand for wheat');
(b) 1/40 is the ratio of natural resources;
(c) 1/60 is the ratio of wheat input coefficients;
(d) 6 is the land-wheat input coefficient; while
(e) 1/0·94 is the 'grossing-up' ratio to provide the profit margin.
As expected, a rise in (a), (b), (d) or (e) or a fall in (c) will raise the price of wheat.

are in the nature of additional details to be added to our description of a productive system, the picture of which in general outline is already clearly drawn. The reader will by now have noted as a major characteristic of the system the interdependence of the several industries which results from their use of common resources and of one another's products.*

If the smallness of the number of industries in our examples above be thought to give the argument an air of unreality, the reader may usefully set up and compute further examples containing as many industries as he may choose. The frontispiece (Table 1) can assist him in choosing industries and institutional data for such an exercise, the method of using the data has been detailed in the previous sections, and the final solution may always be conveniently set out in the form of a transactions table.†

However, the most useful exercise is to set up an example, solve it, and then, by changing some one piece of the institutional data, observe the change in the resulting solution. For example, we may observe the effect of a given increase in the efficiency of the timber-getting industry upon the price of dried fish. Or again we may note the effect of a given increase in population (relatively to the available land) upon the real wage. Such analysis of the effect of a given change in institutional data upon the rest of the productive system is the standard equilibrium problem of positive economics.‡

In conclusion, the distinguishing characteristic of the productive systems analysed in this chapter is the fixity of ratios. The quantity of resources available for productive activity (and hence the ratio of resources employed to resources idle) is fixed; the ratio in which factors are combined in producing a good is fixed; the ratio in which consumers demand commodities is fixed; and so on. So long as these ratios are all fixed, it is easy to follow how resources are absorbed into industries which in turn produce consumer-goods in a steady flow. If any such ratio is not fixed by the environment, then the ratio to be used is a matter for choice. When the ratio has been chosen, it is then adopted, and the productive system operates to all intents and purposes just as if that particular ratio had been fixed in the first place. The

* This interdependence becomes yet more marked when opportunities for choice are introduced so that, for example, inventions in the electricity industry, by lowering its price, increase the demand for electric power at the expense of the competing gas industry, whose output declines. It is because the present method of analysis examines both the overall operation of the productive system (and so is 'general') and the interdependence of all sectors or industries that the analysis is labelled 'the theory of general interdependence'. Inasmuch as we are presently concerned with ascertaining equilibrium levels of output, the analysis may be termed 'general equilibrium'.

† Much of the tedium of solving the system can be avoided by the use of determinants, a most felicitous discussion of which is contained in W. F. Osgood and W. C. Graustein, *Plane and Solid Analytical Geometry*.

‡ Normative economics, on the other hand, asks *by what means* a particular effect upon the productive system may be brought about. There are frequently several such means of achieving a given effect.

16

rest of this essay, then, is concerned to supplement the argument of this chapter in this single respect: if there is a choice as between alternatives, we shall show which will be chosen*—the system of production will then operate precisely as if this alternative had been institutionally ordained and the other alternatives had not existed. For example, the wheat-farmer may have a choice as regards the ratio in which he employs labour and land, or the steelmaster as regards the ratio in which he uses dolomite and manganiferous ore—we shall show in Chapter IV that in these cases the ratio chosen is specified by the simple criterion called the equi-marginal productivity condition.

* We shall find that this comprises one or both of two problems. First, is the ratio positive finite? Second, if so, what is the numerical value of the ratio? We can frequently answer the first question in the affirmative by mere inspection and then proceed to the second question, which is usually solved by a routine procedure (for example see Chapter IV). Occasionally, too, we can answer the first question in the negative merely by inspection of alternatives—for example, in a process where zinc and copper are perfectly substitutable for one another, the choice of which metal will be used (i.e. whether the ratio of zinc to copper used will be zero or infinity) will be determined directly by which is the cheaper. However, in ascertaining the choice between alternative production functions (including the choice of alternative locations) it may not always be possible to solve the first question by inspection and in this case each alternative possibility must be explored in detail—for example, if there are two methods of producing steel (or two places at which steel could be produced!) then either one or both might be used. Each of these three possibilities must be analysed and only the one(s) will be used which can sell a positive output at a competitive price.

17

CHAPTER II

THE LEVEL OF ACTIVITY

§1. The main course of the argument will be resumed in Chapter IV. For the present let us review the overall operation of the system of production. Clearly there is an ultimate physical limit to the possible output at any time—and this is set by the amount of resources in existence. However, the output of the entire system may be less than this ultimate limit for either of two reasons. First, as idle factors can be a direct source of satisfaction to their owners (e.g. idle labour, park-land), some factors may not be available for

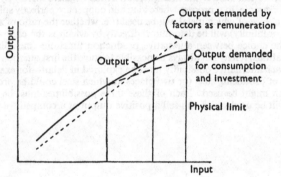

Fig. 11. The limit to production is set in *one* of the three ways indicated.

rent to firms or farms or at least may demand a rental so large that it would not be paid, and so those factors are not employed. However, in our present society owners of factors rarely limit production in this fashion. Alternatively (and this *is* an important limit), people seeking to allocate their income so as to maximize satisfaction may not spend all their income, and if, at the level of maximum production, their savings are not entirely devoted to the purchase of buildings, machinery and other investment goods then there will be an accumulation of unsold stocks equal to the unspent portion of income. As a result the level of output will be reduced until firms find that sales are equal to current production. This can be expressed quite simply in a diagram (Fig. 11). It is characteristic of a 'depression' that the level of output is limited by the level of demand, whereas, when prosperity develops, output is finally limited by the physical scarcity of resources (and indeed also by the willingness of workers to work additional hours for overtime rates). We may also observe that when we know that demand is limiting output we can ascertain equilibrium output without knowing exactly what total resources exist, whereas

18

when resources limit output we can, if we know all demand functions but one, determine the output of the remaining consumer-good as the 'residual' of what the total resources can produce.

§2. As we are shortly to analyse the effect of economizing decisions on the level of production, it may be stressed here that the nature of these decisions is independent of the type of productive system—they are the same for Robinson Crusoe as for John Doe. The method of giving effect to such decisions is affected, however—as when the individual determines the composition of production, not directly by allocating his labour between wheat and cloth production but indirectly by allocating his money income in the purchase of these commodities. This difference in method may be important, and in demonstrating how production is determined it will later be found useful to distinguish three types of exchange, viz. of factor-services (or goods produced by factors) exchanged: for other goods (i.e. barter); for money to be spent currently; for money whose expenditure is deferred.

Before proceeding, it must be added that the scope for individual economizing activity is partly determined by tradition. In this sense any model we construct is institutional and hence not general.* Various national systems of production exist in which the scope for economizing activity is determined by religion, by a tradition of communal effort, by a desire to avoid change, by a desire to use up-to-date production methods, by an inherited or indoctrinated preference for leisure rather than material goods (and conversely). These traditions are a dominant element in the productive life of nations, setting as they do a constraint upon decisions to produce.

* Cf. J. A. Schumpeter, *Business Cycles*, p. 144.

CHAPTER III

THE PRODUCTION FUNCTION

§1. The production function is of such importance that further consideration must be given to it before proceeding to the analysis of economizing activity. As already stated, the production function of a plant is the relation between the rate of input of factors and the rate of output of commodities, such that, given the state of technical knowledge and any technically fixed inputs, the function expresses the maximum product obtainable from any combination of variable factors.* Four points may be made to clarify this definition. First, the production function refers strictly to a process of production. However, we shall use it wherever possible to refer to a set of consecutive processes. Second, the function refers not only to a process or set of processes but also to a particular method of production—for example, the process of shaping a car-body may be carried out by means of panel-beating or by power press. Third, the function may be narrowly defined, not with respect to the firm or industry, but with respect to a plant or plant-entity. A plant-entity is a group of productive inputs operating independently and hence is the unit with respect to which are made decisions concerning what to produce and what combinations of inputs to use. However, we shall usually define the function with the broader reference to the firm or industry, and in particular we shall for convenience assume wherever possible that the plant-entity is identical with the firm. Fourth, the plant-entity is usually associated with equipment and services whose rate of input is invariant over the entire range of the plant's output—or at least the relevant portion of its range. The function is defined with reference to these fixed inputs—which in practice mainly refer to investment goods and administrative services. Since, however, fixity not of physical input but of cost is significant for the profit-maximizing objective, attention may have to be paid to inputs satisfying only the second of these criteria.†

§2. In order to ascertain possible forms of the firm's production function it is convenient to consider the properties of the function under four

* Cf. S. Carlson, *A Study on the Pure Theory of Production*, p. 14. 'Maximum production' here refers to the technical problem of getting the most out of a given group of factors. We define as *the same factor* all inputs which are both physically identical and have the same price. In the case of labour, 'physical identity' is interpreted to mean membership of the genus 'man'.

† As a general comment it may be added that if the expansion of output beyond critical levels required a change in plant processes or in the physical nature of inputs, the production function would take the form of a series of relations referring to the several ranges of output.

heads: the significance of resources which are exhausted by use; the effect on output of varying the rate of input of a single factor in a productive combination; the effect on output of varying proportionately the rate of input of all factors in a productive combination; elements limiting the firm's size.

Exhausting resources

Consider the significance for input-output relations of the use of the services of exhausting resources. Whether or not such resources are irreplaceable may not be known. But for our purpose the industries using these resources may be classified as either extractive or primary producing—the latter depending in part upon the existence of living matter in the process of production.

In the primary producing industries the production function is not normally of the form which shows a unique relation between the current rates of input and the current rate of output. Rather, the characteristic situation is that the current rates of input determine not only the current rate of output but also the period for which that rate of output can be obtained. In other words, some high value of the rate of input of factors will not produce its initial (high) rate of output for as long a period as some lower value of the rate of input will produce its initial (lower) rate of output—the reason being that the higher rate of input involves a greater rate of physical exhaustion of resources. Finally, at some lower rate of input the initial rate of output might be capable of being maintained indefinitely* because resources are regularly rehabilitated. These propositions apply to the rate of grazing of livestock per unit of land; to the rate of cropping a unit of land both by intensive cultivation and by frequency of harvesting; to the rate of killing of birds, animals and fish in their natural habitats; and to the rate of cutting of forests.

In discussing primary industries there is a second problem closely connected with the first, viz. that the production functions of various outputs are not independent. This point is best grasped by conceiving of the notion of balance in natural life—a balance which may be altered by man's activities. First, for example, animals may be killed which prey on rodents, or birds which prey on destructive insects, or vegetation may be cropped or destroyed which is essential to the life-cycle of insects which assist man. A second example is that the rate of cutting of forests affects soil erosion as well as the total volume and depth of the upper level of underground water resources—and through these the production functions of other primary industry are affected, even to the location or survival of the community.

Consider now the extractive industries—the other group at the apex of the vertical structure of industry. Minerals cannot at present be replaced and there are limits to the use of 'waste-products'. This shrinkage of resources

---

* If this is not possible, it follows that useful resources are shrinking continuously—save in so far as invention and ingenuity find use for resources hitherto ignored.

21

tends to reduce the social product—an effect which can only be offset by increasing technical knowledge (both as regards more efficient productive organization of factors and as regards uses for hitherto unused resources) or from the resources of living organisms—for example, if forests could be increased to produce synthetics in substitution for metals.

Solely as a measure of simplification, we shall in the rest of this chapter abstract entirely from the problems stated in the last three paragraphs: we shall assume that production functions are independent of one another and that their time-span is unlimited. However, these critical assumptions must not be forgotten in any practical application of the study.

Individual input variation

Any variation of inputs falls under one of the following heads: individual variation of one factor (or factor-group), other inputs being unchanged; or 'scale' (i.e. equi-proportional) variation of all inputs. The following examination of the possible effects on output of these two variations is intended to throw light on the possible form of the function.

Consider the case of individual variation. The problem is to know how the marginal product* of the factor varies as its input is increased, all other inputs being invariant. There are the following possibilities: The marginal product may be either zero or positive. If positive and continuous, the marginal product might logically be constant or increasing, but we may assume that in practice it will (saving more complex oscillations) either decrease monotonically or pass through one or both of the successive phases of increase and constancy before decreasing.

There are then three main possibilities regarding the values which the marginal product may assume. Light may also be thrown on the properties of the production function by considering how a change in the input of one factor affects the marginal rate of substitution between two variable factors— the latter being defined as the reciprocal of the ratio of the marginal productivities of the factors. This technical marginal rate of substitution may be constant (including zero and unity as special cases) or variable, for example, such that the marginal rate of substitution of y for x diminishes as the input of factor x alone increases.

Scale input variation

Consider now the effect upon output of simultaneous equi-proportional increase of all variable inputs. We examine this property of the production function for two reasons. The obvious one is that we wish to know the possible

---

* If the input of a factor is measured in a sufficiently small unit of quantity, the *marginal product* of the factor is the addition to total output resulting from a unit increase in the input of the factor. For a further discussion see Appendix I, p. 94.

form of the function, e.g. whether the firm is of constant scale efficiency.*
The second is that we wish to know whether the form of the firm's production
function is such that the aggregate production function for all firms producing the commodity (i.e. the industry production function) is invariant with
respect to the size of such firms—or, in other words, if the same quantity of
factors continued to be employed in the entire industry but were employed
by (for example) half the number of firms, whether the total output of
the industry would be the same. From the viewpoint of practical investigation, this property of invariance will later be found to be of paramount
importance.

The course of the discussion is then as follows: The hypothesis is advanced
that the elasticity of firm's output with respect to equi-proportional increase
of all variable inputs is unity, i.e. the firm is of constant scale efficiency. (This
is consistent with the invariance of the aggregate function with respect to
firm size.) The immediate problem is to consider possible causes of divergence
from such unit elasticity (or 'constant scale return').† In each case we consider whether there is any inconsistency with the invariance of the aggregate
(or industry) function with respect to firm size.

One possible cause of divergence is that the direction and management of
a business firm and its commercial relations may become more difficult as
the firm expands. However, increasing size may equally bring with it the
introduction of large-scale management techniques and increasing managerial
specialization which permit almost indefinite expansion without loss of
efficiency.‡ Two comments may be made, neither of which lends support to
the former contention. First, contrary to the view that entrepreneurship is
a 'fixed' input, practical experience suggests that entrepreneurial effort by
nature approximates rather to a variable input—the volume of planning,
directing and co-ordinating staff being increased with the level of activity.
This suggests that the personal limitations of the entrepreneur do not cause
diminishing scale return and thereby determine the level of firm's output.
Second, an outstanding characteristic of industry is the co-existence of small,
medium and large firms. This, though by no means conclusive, is consistent
with the view that management is of constant efficiency and hence that the
aggregate function is invariant with respect to the size of the firms in the
industry.§

* I.e. whether, say, doubling all inputs results in double the output.
† The common usage of 'constant scale return' is highly equivocal, since the elasticity
may be constant at a figure other than unity.
‡ Cf. P. W. S. Andrews, 'A Reconsideration of the Theory of the Individual Business',
Oxford Economic Papers, 1949, pp. 69–71.
§ It is not intended to decide the issue by counting pros and cons. Clearly an entrepreneur's personal inability may determine his firm's output. What is intended is to cast
strong doubt on the reasonableness of this as a *general* cause of diminishing scale return
and as an explanation of the popular U-shape of the firm's cost curve.

A second possible cause of divergence is that the efficiency of the firm's productive combination may alter because of size (management of constant efficiency being assumed). There are three possibilities to consider here. First, genuine 'economies or diseconomies of scale' of a purely organizational character may well exist, although it would be difficult to urge that these phenomena are very widespread. Second, the efficiency of the productive combination may decline because of the diminishing efficiency of labour (whether because the same workers are less efficient as longer hours are worked or because successively less efficient workers are employed). Labour is here singled out for consideration because it alone of all factors is paid a given time-rate irrespective of efficiency. However, it is doubtful whether firms do in general find labour to be of diminishing efficiency with scale expansion. On the other hand, it is possibly a characteristic of the firm-system* where men work with equipment which is not owned by them, that production per man may fall as the general level of employment expands— and this because of the goad of unemployment. To affirm this, however, is to affirm that efficiency depends on the level of activity in general (or even in the industry). It does not conflict with the view that the aggregate production function is invariant with respect to the size of the firm. Third, it may appear that the efficiency of the productive combination may decline because of the diminishing efficiency of some other factor. This is fallacious: the essence of the notion of, say, diminishing scale returns is not that different, less efficient, factors must be used, but that expanded use of the same factors involves a less efficient combination. Thus the expansion of production may draw into use less fertile and less accessible land, less pure and less accessible mineral deposits. This diminishing fertility is not, however, a cause of diminishing scale returns, for these are different factors.

A third possible cause of divergence is that some factors may be indivisible. Whereas inputs such as land, chemicals, raw materials generally and even labour may be regarded as infinitely divisible, this is not the case for many other factors. Two cases may be conveniently distinguished. The first is typified by the nickel mine or coal mine where variable inputs are applied to a fixed natural resource. It is clearly possible that diminishing returns to scale may be met simply because scale expansion may necessitate digging deeper. However, it is submitted that such diminishing returns are a result of the expansion of the industry and not of the firm. Deeper mines are required because the entire industry is pressing against available natural resources. In the mining example the view is again advanced that the aggregate function is invariant with respect to the size of the firm. The second case is

---

* To call it the 'factory system' is to give an unduly narrow definition. The firm-system owes its existence largely to the increased opportunities it offers for specialization and hence greater production.

24

typified by the example of the tractor, the plant generator or the factory building. When a unit of such a factor is introduced, there is a range of expansion of output over which the services of this input are not fully utilized. This means that constant proportional scale returns, assuming they would exist in the absence of the lumpiness of the factor, are discontinuous— so that every time the normal capacity of the lumpy factor is reached, the current output will lie on the curve of constant proportional return. But how does output vary between these points? The importance of this question can be exaggerated—in fact the discontinuities are often small relative to output and then the lumpy factors can conveniently be regarded as divisible.

However, there certainly are cases where the discontinuities may be large— so large as to embrace the entire output of the firm. In such case, to answer the question we refer back to the discussion of changes in marginal productivity, and the point is most clearly seen if we imagine the two-factor case, one being fixed (by virtue of its lumpiness)* and the other variable over the range of output considered. The previous assertion holds, that the marginal product of the variable factor or factor-group will (fixed proportions being excluded) either decrease monotonically or pass through one or both of the successive phases of increase and constancy before decreasing. The latter alternative alone is consistent with the requirement that, at normal capacity of the lumpy factor, output shall lie on the curve of constant scale return. Under this alternative, increasing marginal productivity of the variable input might conceivably result from the initially better exploitation of the fixed input, which at some stage gives way to relative limitation of the fixed input resulting in declining marginal productivity. However, probably the most important case included under this alternative is that where marginal productivity is constant over the range, being then followed by an abrupt decline at normal capacity. In this case, output remains throughout on the curve of constant proportional return.†

A fourth apparent cause of divergence is that increase in size may bring with it the opportunity for increasing the degree of mechanization in production. In general, more extensive specialization is possible as output expands. It may accordingly be suggested that size brings increasing returns to scale in terms of the inputs required—directly and indirectly to produce specialized equipment—to produce the output. However, the fact is that different methods

---

* The rate of input of the lumpy factor is fixed over a range of output because of the requirement, laid down in the definition of the production function, that from any given combination of inputs, maximum output shall be obtained. This can only be technically satisfied if the input is fixed over the range.

† In passing, it is interesting that it is extraordinarily difficult to think of a lumpy factor which does not outlast the period of production. Although it is not logically necessary, it appears that all lumpy factors are also investment goods. We shall later make use of this observation.

of production are under consideration—the introduction of a new machine involves the consideration of a new production function.*

The above discussion is consistent with the view that characteristically the aggregate production function of the industry is invariant with respect to the size of the firms producing the commodity.† The truth of this hypothesis, of course, depends on more considerations than have so far been raised and in any event can only be decided by practical investigation. Henceforth in this essay we shall employ this hypothesis, and its use enables us to drop the assumption that the industry is directed by a single board of management—for by this hypothesis, the output obtainable from a given group of factors will be the same irrespective of whether the industry is controlled by one firm or by ten (the normal profit condition being the same in both cases). As regards the precise form of the firm's production function, which is the first consideration of this chapter, it may now be suggested that frequently, although certainly not necessarily, the elasticity of output with respect to scale variation of all inputs is unity.

Size limitation

Some elements which may limit the size of the firm have already been indicated expressly or by implication. Two, however, are of particular import. It is frequently the case that the firm produces a commodity which is not perfectly substitutable, in the purchaser's estimation, with any other commodity. Because of this 'differentiation' of the product there is a limit to the size of demand for a firm's output. But of all limiting elements probably none is of more general significance than the difficulty of obtaining command over productive resources. For the entrepreneur must at least have sufficient capital—whether in material form or in monetary claims on the social product —to pay for current inputs of labour and materials before he is able to sell his product. The problem is, of course, that there is a limit both to the amount of capital he possesses himself and to the amount he can borrow.

§3. In review, the analysis of the properties of the firm's production function has made the following points:

(1) Exhausting resources may affect the form of the function.
(2) The marginal product of a factor may
    (i) be zero;
    (ii) decrease monotonically;
    (iii) pass through one or both of the successive phases of increase and constancy before decreasing.

* This apart, however, the existence of two such production functions within the technological horizon of the firm is a cause of instability. Hence it is reasonable to conduct our discussion of equilibrium on the assumption that, if the horizon is of this nature, adjustment to a stable position has already been attained.

† Characteristically, the expansion of an industry proceeds by reduplication of existing plants.

(3) Scale returns may be of unit elasticity, although divergence from this is conceivable for a variety of causes.

(4) Limits to the size of the firm are set notably by product differentiation and by the difficulty of obtaining command over resources.

§4.* As a step towards later quantitative analysis, we shall now consider briefly a few function types having the properties set out above.

First, consider a production function of the following form (X measures physical output; x, y, z are the physical inputs of respective factors; a, b, h, j, k, m, n, p are constants):

$$X = a \cdot x^h \cdot y^j \cdot z^k + b \cdot x^m \cdot y^n \cdot z^p + \dots$$

The right-hand side of the expression may or may not be homogeneous. In the homogeneous case, the sum of the indices ($h+j+k=m+n+p=\dots$) may be equal to or greater or less than unity, corresponding respectively to constant, increasing and decreasing proportional returns to scale.

The marginal productivity of any factor is immediately derived by partial differentiation.† In the homogeneous one-term function, $X = a \cdot x^h \cdot y^j \cdot z^k$,

$$\frac{\partial X}{\partial x} = \frac{h}{x} \cdot X, \quad \frac{\partial^2 X}{\partial x^2} = \frac{h(h-1)}{x^2} \cdot X, \quad \text{and} \quad \frac{\partial^2 X}{\partial y \partial x} = \frac{h \cdot j}{x \cdot y} \cdot X.‡$$

Hence, so long as the exponent of x is positive and less than unity, the marginal productivity of x is positive and is decreasing as the input of x alone increases. Further, so long as the exponents of the other inputs are positive (which includes the case where they are also less than unity), then the marginal productivity of x is increasing as the input of another factor alone increases.

Secondly, consider the function

$$X = a \cdot \frac{x^2}{y} - b \cdot \frac{x^3}{y^2},$$

which is the simplest formulation of the homogeneous linear case where marginal productivity of a factor rises and falls with a change in the ratio of the inputs. Examine now the marginal productivity of x, and the symbol y may be taken to represent either another homogeneous input or a group of inputs.

$$\frac{\partial X}{\partial x} = 2a \cdot \frac{x}{y} - 3b \cdot \frac{x^2}{y^2}, \text{ which } \gtreqless 0 \text{ according as } \frac{2a}{3b} \gtreqless \frac{x}{y}.$$

$$\frac{\partial}{\partial \left(\frac{x}{y} \right)} \left(\frac{\partial X}{\partial x} \right) = 2a - 6b \cdot \frac{x}{y}, \text{ which } \gtreqless 0 \text{ according as } \frac{a}{3b} \gtreqless \frac{x}{y}.$$

* The reader who eschews algebra may omit this section if he chooses. The level of analysis is elementary, however, and he is urged to read Appendix I before proceeding.

† See Appendix I, p. 94.

‡ For the homogeneous one-term function, $X \gtreqless \sum\limits_{x}^{z} \frac{\partial X}{\partial x} \cdot x$ according as the sum of the indices is less than, equal to, or greater than unity.

27

So the marginal productivity of x, which is positive so long as $\frac{x}{y} < \frac{2}{3} \cdot \frac{a}{b}$, is increasing as $\frac{x}{y}$ increases so long as $\frac{x}{y} < \frac{1}{3} \cdot \frac{a}{b}$ and is thereafter decreasing. In similar fashion, it is seen that the marginal productivity of y, which is positive so long as $\frac{x}{y} > \frac{1}{2} \cdot \frac{a}{b}$, is increasing as $\frac{x}{y}$ increases so long as $\frac{x}{y} > \frac{1}{3} \cdot \frac{a}{b}$. The significant point of the discussion is that in practice the ratio of inputs must lie within the limits

$$\frac{1}{2} \cdot \frac{a}{b} < \frac{x}{y} < \frac{2}{3} \cdot \frac{a}{b},$$

as outside these limits the marginal productivity of a factor is negative. This puts in formal terms the simple idea that beyond a point the continued relative increase of one input may be detrimental to the efficiency of the inputs already in use.

The third case requiring mention is that of fixed proportions. If returns to scale are constant, we have

$$X = a.x = b.y = c.z,$$

where the marginal productivity of all factors is clearly zero.

Whether the above types of function exist and, if so, whether they are of general importance, are questions only to be answered by empirical investigation. But for the present we shall feel justified in the ensuing chapters in assuming the existence of one or other or combinations of these forms.

CHAPTER IV

FACTOR SUBSTITUTION
(SECOND MODEL)

§ 1. The institutional data of Chapter I, §3, are now relaxed to admit a single opportunity for economizing decision to appear: it is assumed that factors of production may be technically substitutable in production. For example, the wheat farmer may be able, while reducing the area sown, to produce the same amount of wheat by labouring on its cultivation more intensively—a substitution of labour for land. In short, the farmer or business-man now has a choice as to the ratio in which he will employ his factors of production. His choice is guided by the objective of maximum profit, and the ratio he chooses must satisfy the condition:*

The ratio of the marginal product of a factor to that factor's price shall be the same for all factors, i.e.

$$\frac{\text{Marg. prod. of } x}{\text{Price of } x} = \frac{\text{Marg. prod. of } y}{\text{Price of } y} = \frac{\text{Marg. prod. of } z}{\text{Price of } z} = \dots,$$

where x, y, z are factors of production.

This necessary maximum condition† is known as the *equi-marginal productivity condition* since it states that the output per £ spent on a factor must be equal at the margin for all factors. It is clear that for any given set of factor prices there is a corresponding ratio in which the factors will be employed since the entrepreneur seeks to satisfy the condition of equi-marginal productivity—so long as he is *not* satisfying the condition, it is always possible for him to produce a greater output for the same cost.

§ 2. To illustrate factor substitution we shall for brevity consider the case of a single-industry system. It is clear enough that, however many industries there are, the farmer or businessman will seek to satisfy the equi-marginal productivity condition if substitution between inputs is possible.

Consider then a productive system where:

The labour force is 10,000 men and the quantity of land is 900,000 acres, both factors being available at whatever price they can obtain;

---

* In Appendix II (p. 98) the procedure for ascertaining the necessary condition for a maximum is stated. The procedure is applied to the present case in the *Note* to Chapter XI, p. 73, where this equi-marginal productivity condition is formally derived.

† The necessary maximum condition is of this simple form both when all factor prices are constant and also under a wider set of conditions. We postpone a fuller statement until Chapter XI.

The sole productive activity is wheat farming, the production function of the industry being

$$X_w = \frac{x_{nw}^2}{x_{lw}} - 50 \cdot \frac{x_{nw}^3}{x_{lw}^2}$$

where X_w is wheat output (hundred-thousand bushels), x_{nw} is labour input (man-years) and x_{lw} the input of land (acres);*

The normal profit rate of wheat farms is 8 % of the value of output;

Consumers spend their entire income, there being no saving;

The sole demand for money being to carry out transactions, this demand is given by

$$M_{TC} = 0.07 X_w \cdot P_w,$$

where P_w is the price of wheat. The supply of money from the banking system is £500,000.

Consider first the total level of output. The level of activity is limited neither by consumer-demand nor by reservation price on factor supply. Since from the production function we observe that land and labour must be used together in a ratio within the range

$$\frac{1}{100} < \frac{x_{nw}}{x_{lw}} < \frac{1}{75},$$

it follows that the level of output is here limited only by the physical quantity of resources, all men and land being employed (in the ratio $1:90$) to produce an output of 49·48 hundred-thousand bushels. As the transactions demand for money is known, it follows further that the price of wheat will be £1·44643 per bushel.

Now we know that the ratio of prices of land and labour must equal the ratio of their marginal products; and the marginal product of labour is $\frac{1}{270}$ hundred-thousand bushels and that of land is $\frac{1}{72900}$ hundred-thousand bushels. Hence from the profit and loss account (or cost equation) we find that the rent of land is £1·8254 per acre and the wage-rate is £492·76 per year.

These results are conveniently summarized in Table 5.

It is true, as the reader may object, that it is only by examining movement *from one equilibrium to another* that one appreciates the effect of substitution or economizing decisions. Suppose, therefore, that in the above society land-owners decide they will only rent land at a minimum or 'reservation' price of £2 an acre (instead of, as before, at any price they can get). This price rise will cause a 'substitution effect', inasmuch as farmers will employ more labour

---

* The two major characteristics of this function are: the industry is of constant scale efficiency; labour and land must be employed at a ratio within the range 1/75 to 1/100, i.e. factor substitution is possible but within limits.

per acre. In fact, while continuing to employ the entire work force, only 892·9 thousand acres will be used in wheat production and the remainder will be idle.*

Table 5. *Transactions during twelvemonth*

Output of	Price (£)	Sold to (£m.)	
		1	Consumers
1. Wheat (bushel)	1·446	—	7·15
2. Labour (men)	493·0	4·93	—
3. Land (acre)	1·825	1·65	—
4. Profit	—	0·57	—
Value added	—	7·15	—

* The student can compute this result if he has had the most elementary experience of quadratic equations. It is a simple matter to use this 892·9 in order to work out, as before, the remaining quantities and prices and set them out in tabular form.

CHAPTER V

CONSUMPTION
(THIRD MODEL)

§1. A further opportunity for economizing activity is now introduced by the recognition that individuals may purchase one consumer-good instead of another, if their relative prices vary.* So, whereas in Chapter I it was assumed that the quantity of, say, butter purchased for consumption was determined solely by the individual's income, we now recognize that it is determined not alone by income but also by the price of butter, as well as by the price of such a closely competing good as margarine and by the prices of all the other commodities which the individual purchases (and which compete on a price basis for the allocation of the individual's income). For if the cost of producing, and so the price of butter, rose we should expect a transfer of demand away from butter in favour of other commodities whose prices were unchanged.

This new development is most simply introduced into the system of relations which describe the productive system. It is now merely necessary that the consumer-demand function for each final commodity be stated in the form already set out on p. 6, i.e.

Quantity demanded is a function of $\begin{cases} \text{income;} \\ \text{own price;} \\ \text{prices of other consumer-goods.} \end{cases}$

Indeed, this is all the theoretical equipment needed to proceed to practical analysis where the prime problem is the statistical one of actually specifying the form of and the numbers in the consumption function. However, it is possible to some extent to 'go behind' this behaviour function and in particular to show how it expresses the actions taken by the individual as a result of economizing choice. This we shall do in the following sections.

§2. The marginal utility of any commodity x to an individual is defined as the increase in total utility or satisfaction obtained from consumption which results from increasing his consumption of x by one unit.† Using this definition, we make the following basic assertion as to the nature of individual tastes:

The marginal utility of any consumption good x to the individual (is positive and) diminishes as the intake of x increases, all other intakes remaining unchanged.

* It is, of course, tacitly assumed that at least one common factor is involved in the production of the various goods—else there could be no meaning to the term 'economizing'.

† The unit is a physical one and must be sufficiently small. The definition is precisely parallel to that of marginal product (see Appendix I).

The reader may object that this is a rather formal way of saying that 'variety is the spice of life' but from our present point of view, another objection may be raised. For, since utility can be neither observed nor measured, the assertion is about something with which it is difficult to come to grips. Some progress can be made in overcoming this difficulty by introducing the concept of the marginal rate of substitution of commodity y for commodity x (briefly denoted as m.r.s.$_{y/x}$), which is defined as: the quantity of commodity y the individual is prepared to give in order to obtain an additional unit of commodity x.* The advantage of this concept is that it refers to market activity and it is at least conceivable that we should be able to watch the individual's market operations in order to ascertain his marginal rate of substitution. However, it is not immediately obvious that we can deduce from the basic assertion the further statement:

m.r.s.$_{y/x}$ diminishes as the intake of x increases, all other intakes remaining unchanged.

For the two commodities may be competing, independent or complementary, in which case the 'cross effects' on utility between x and y are respectively negative, zero and positive. For example, if they are competing, an increase in x not only lowers the marginal utility of x but also lowers that of y, and since by definition m.r.s.$_{y/x}$ equals the ratio of their marginal utilities (m.u.$_x$/m.u.$_y$), there seems no way of knowing whether m.r.s.$_{y/x}$ has fallen or risen. It is this common case of competing or substitutable goods having negative cross effects that obstructs the argument. The difficulty is best resolved by examining the extreme case where x and y are perfect substitutes and hence indefinitely substitutable in fixed proportions. As the ratio of their marginal utilities is then by definition constant, the negative cross effects must be sufficiently large exactly to offset effects on own utility. But in all other cases, since the degree of substitution is less, the negative cross effects must be less than this and hence there is a fall in the ratio of marginal utilities (m.u.$_x$/m.u.$_y$) as x increases, and so by definition a fall in m.r.s.$_{y/x}$, the number of units of y which compensate for a unit of x. Hence the deduction can be made for all cases save the limiting one of perfect substitution.†

It will be seen that individual's tastes may be represented by stating the value of the m.r.s. between each pair of commodities as a function of his rate

* The units are physical and the unit of measurement of x must again be small, since we want to measure the *rate* of substitution at the margin, i.e. at a point.

† The argument can be extended to obtain a further result. By an argument symmetrical to that in the text we can also show that m.r.s.$_{y/x}$ increases (i.e. m.r.s.$_{x/y}$ decreases) as the intake of y increases, all other intakes remaining unchanged. Now from this proposition and the symmetrical one in the text we can deduce that m.r.s.$_{y/x}$ diminishes as the intake of x increases and the intake of y is decreased so as to leave the individual in an equally preferred position (all other intakes remaining unchanged). For if he is indifferent as between two collections of goods where only the quantities of x and y are different, one

of intake of each consumer-good.* The main characteristic of this substitution function (viz. diminishing m.r.s.) has been stated. We may now state the necessary maximum condition which the individual must satisfy to be in his equilibrium position of greatest satisfaction. This condition is perfectly analogous to the equi-marginal productivity(/utility) condition and states that the ratio of the marginal utility of a commodity to its price is the same for all commodities—for if this condition is not satisfied the individual can always increase his satisfaction by making a switch in expenditure.† This condition can be restated in the form: in equilibrium the marginal rate of substitution between any two commodities equals the reciprocal of the ratio of their prices, i.e.

$$\text{m.r.s.}_{y/x} = \frac{P_x}{P_y}, \quad \text{m.r.s.}_{z/x} = \frac{P_x}{P_z}, \quad \text{m.r.s.}_{w/x} = \frac{P_x}{P_w},$$

or more briefly,

$$\text{m.r.s.}_{y/x} \cdot P_y = \text{m.r.s.}_{z/x} \cdot P_z = \text{m.r.s.}_{w/x} \cdot P_w = P_x.$$

A second condition is that the value of the individual's goods (or his income) before he spends them in exchange for other goods, equals the value of all his goods (including any residue of income) after the exchange, i.e. he receives in proportion to what he gives:

$$P_x(x - x_0) + P_y(y - y_0) + P_z(z - z_0) + P_w(w - w_0) = 0,$$

where the subscript zero indicates original quantities possessed and x, y, z, w are the quantities possessed on any subsequent occasion, for example after having spent one's income (say w_0) on consumer-goods. This second condition is sometimes called the 'budget constraint': it stresses that you cannot spend more than your income. The equi-marginal utility condition determines the *ratio* in which goods are demanded; the budget constraint determines the scale of aggregate consumption expenditure.

collection must contain more of x and less of y than another, i.e. in the diagram, collection B is below and to the right of collection A.

But we know that m.r.s.$_{y/x}$ is greater at A than at C and is greater at C than at B. So m.r.s.$_{y/x}$ declines as we proceed from A to B which are but two of the many points on an indifference curve.

* Tastes may also be represented by a utility function or an index function.

† The reader familiar with total derivatives (see G. W. Caunt, *Infinitesimal Calculus*, p. 488) can formally derive this equi-marginal utility condition as a necessary condition for maximum satisfaction. See, for example, R. G. D. Allen, *Mathematical Analysis for Economists* (London, 1949), p. 374.

Consider these two sets of equilibrium conditions. If we know tastes, then each of the marginal rates of substitution, m.r.s.$_{y/x}$, m.r.s.$_{z/x}$, m.r.s.$_{w/x}$, is known as determined by the rates of intake. If x_0, y_0, z_0, w_0 are also known (e.g. w_0 may be a given income and $x_0 = y_0 = z_0 = 0$), then for any given set of prices P_x, P_y, P_z, P_w we can immediately determine the quantities x, y, z, w and so the equilibrium quantities $(x - x_0)$, $(y - y_0)$... which the individual will demand at those prices. But we can do this for *any* set of prices. For example, we can deduce the effect of a change in P_y on the demand for y and on the demand for other goods too. In short, from a knowledge of individuals' tastes and of their desire to achieve maximum satisfaction we can deduce the precise numerical form of the consumer-demand function for each commodity.*

§3. Let us consider the properties of the demand function.† If the individual's money income rises, other prices remaining unchanged, his real income has clearly risen. As a result, his demand for individual commodities will change—more of some being demanded and perhaps less of others.‡ If, however, money income is unchanged, while the price of some commodity A falls,§ once again real income of the individual has risen. But also the relative prices of commodities have altered. Consequently in this case consumption demand is affected in two ways—there is a 'real income' effect and a 'substitution' effect. So long as no other price changes it follows, from the postulate of diminishing marginal rate of substitution and from the equilibrium condition that the marginal rate of substitution equals the reciprocal of the ratio of prices of any two commodities, that the substitution effect involves an increased quantity purchased of the new cheaper commodity A in preference to other commodities; but we can make no general statement regarding the direction of the real income effect.

Proceeding a step further we may inquire about the effect of such a change in the price of A upon demand for another commodity B. As before, the demand for B is subject to both an income and a substitution effect. This time the direction of the substitution effect is also in doubt. For, as previously noted, the relation between the two commodities may be that of competition, independence or complementarity and demand for B (so far as the substitution effect is concerned) may fall, not change, or rise, respectively.

Returning to the effect of a fall in the price of A upon the quantity of A demanded by consumers, we may observe that if the proportion of the individual's income spent on A is small, then the income effect will be small.

* Instead of deriving the demand function by repetitive solution as above, a more efficient way is detailed in H. Schultz, *Theory and Measurement of Demand*, ch. I.

† An important group property of consumer-demand functions will also be considered below (p. 48).

‡ The so-called 'inferior' goods (over the range in question).

§ The initiating cause of price change is likely to be important. Suppose a more efficient method of production is the cause.

CONSUMPTION

In this case therefore, even if the income effect operates in the opposite direction to the substitution effect, it will be insufficiently large to outweigh the substitution effect. Hence where the income effect is small, we have the result that a fall in the price of a consumer-good leads to a rise in the amount of it demanded by consumers, all other prices remaining unchanged.*

This consideration of properties of the demand function, even if we were to go further and consider also elasticities of demand,† does not permit us to make any precise statement as to the characteristic form of the function. In the final analysis this is a matter for empirical investigation. However, approaching the question of the form of the consumption function in a commonsense way, it may be suggested that though indeed the individual's consumption of a commodity is determined by his money income and by the prices both of itself and of other commodities, none the less these determine his consumption only at one remove, so to speak. For the elements which directly determine his consumption are (as seen by him) his *real* income and the prices of commodities *relatively* to each other. It is perhaps a little unfortunate that 'real income' has no unequivocal meaning—for though we define it as money income divided by a retail price index, it is possible to compute more than one such index with somewhat varying results. But there can be no doubt that individuals have a definite conception of real income and so in reality the statistician's task is to construct a price index which most closely corresponds to that conception.

For example, if there were but two consumer-goods, wheat and fish, the simplest form‡ of the two demand functions would be (where Y is total money incomes and P_π the price index)

$$C_w = a + b \cdot \frac{Y}{P_\pi} + c \cdot \frac{P_f}{P_w};$$

$$C_f = e + f \cdot \frac{Y}{P_\pi} + g \cdot \frac{P_w}{P_f}.$$

* See J. R. Hicks, *Value and Capital*, p. 32.

† The responsiveness of demand to a change in income or in own-price or some other price is measured by the ratio of the percentage change in demand to the percentage change in income or price (the absolute amount of this latter change being small). These are the elasticities of demand. For example, the elasticities of demand with respect to income, own price and other price in the two functions on pp. 6, 7 are respectively:

(i) $b \cdot \frac{Y}{C_i}$; $c \cdot \frac{P_i}{C_i}$; $d \cdot \frac{P_j}{C_i}$;

(ii) b; c; d.

‡ Even this complicates the arithmetic of solution and so, to simplify the example of the next section, we shall use the relationship

$$C_w = a + b \cdot \frac{Y}{P_n} + c \cdot \frac{P_w}{P_n} + d \cdot \frac{P_f}{P_n},$$

where P_n, the wage-rate, is used as numéraire (the prices of all other factors and commodities being measured in terms of the wage-unit).

36

An important characteristic of these functions is that if all income and prices were, say, doubled, consumption would remain the same.*

§4. To illustrate this development in our argument, consider a simple society producing but four commodities. All are consumer-goods and the consumer-demand functions are linear. One (boats) is also an investment good and the level of current investment demand for it is known. The institutional data are as follows:

Factor supply functions

The labour force is 50,000 men and the quantity of land is 1,400,000 acres, both factors being available at whatever price they can obtain.

Production functions

Fishing. The intake of labour is 0·2 man-year per ton of output. The existing fishing fleet is eight boats.

Wheat. The intake of labour is 0·1 man-year per ton of output. The intake of land is 6·0 acres per ton of output.

Timber. The intake of labour is 0·01 man-year per ton of output.

Boats. The intake of labour is 0·25 man-year per boat (standard size). The intake of timber is 2·5 tons per boat (standard size).

Normal profit

The profit rate in each industry is 10 % of the value of output.

Consumption functions†

$$C_f = 1\cdot5\,Y - 0\cdot15 P_f + 0\cdot1 P_w,$$
$$C_w = 4\cdot0\,Y + 0\cdot3 P_f - 0\cdot2 P_w,$$
$$C_t = 10\cdot0\,Y,$$
$$C_b = 0\cdot1\,Y.$$

In addition, current investment demand for the fishing industry is known to be two boats per year and the ruling interest rate is 5 %.‡ All boats have

---

* It may also be noted that if we define
$$P_\pi = bP_w + fP_f$$
and if (a and e being negative),
$$a = g; \quad e = c;$$
then the functions collectively give an aggregate expenditure equal to income.

The 'linear' form of the functions has been given in the text for simplicity only. A 'quadratic' form is perhaps more appropriate in many cases.

† To simplify the arithmetic we here define
$$Y = 1\cdot1 \text{ (land rents + wages + interest receipts).}$$
There is no reason why in practice the empirical relations might not prove to be of just the forms set down above—though the national income is in fact somewhat larger than the Y we use here. All prices (of both factors and commodities) are here measured in wage-units.

‡ For simplicity we shall ignore both working capital and the possibility that the interest rate may affect the level of consumption. As mentioned in the preceding section, all prices are measured in terms of the wage-unit. The determination of the level of investment and of the interest rate (here assumed fixed) is analysed in later chapters.

a four-year life and depreciation provision is made at an even rate over this period.

Following the procedure of Chapter I, §9, we shall first assume that some land will be unemployed and hence land will have a zero price. If this assumption is incorrect we shall find the productive system demanding more land than is available and then the argument must be reworked. Perhaps the simplest way of ascertaining whether labour will be fully employed is to let the investment demand for boats be an unknown to be determined by the available resources (i.e. if there is enough labour left over to produce just two boats we know there will be full employment, but if there is more labour than this then there will be unemployment). Proceeding on this second step then, we have the overall requirement limiting aggregate consumption by the available labour:

$$0 \cdot 2 C_f + 0 \cdot 1 C_w + 0 \cdot 01 C_t + 0 \cdot 275 C_b + 0 \cdot 275 I_b = 50,000.$$

Now from the cost equations of the four industries we deduce respectively the commodity prices (in wage units):

$$P_f = \frac{2}{9} + \frac{2}{2 \cdot 43} \cdot \frac{1}{C_f},$$
$$P_w = \tfrac{1}{9},$$
$$P_t = \tfrac{1}{90},$$
$$P_b = 0 \cdot 3086.$$

These prices may be inserted in the four consumer-demand functions:

$$
\left\{
\begin{aligned}
&C_f = 1 \cdot 5(1 \cdot 1 \times 50,000 \cdot 1234) - 0 \cdot 15\left(\frac{2}{9} + \frac{2}{2 \cdot 43} \cdot \frac{1}{C_f}\right) + \frac{0 \cdot 1}{9}; \\
&C_w = 4 \cdot 0(1 \cdot 1 \times 50,000 \cdot 1234) + 0 \cdot 3\left(\frac{2}{9} + \frac{2}{2 \cdot 43} \cdot \frac{1}{C_f}\right) - \frac{0 \cdot 2}{9}; \\
&C_t = 10 \cdot 0(1 \cdot 1 \times 50,000 \cdot 1234); \\
&C_b = 0 \cdot 1(1 \cdot 1 \times 50,000 \cdot 1234); \text{ while as already noted,} \\
&50,000 = 0 \cdot 2 C_f + 0 \cdot 1 C_w + 0 \cdot 01 C_t + 0 \cdot 275 C_b + 0 \cdot 275 I_b.
\end{aligned}
\right.
$$

From these five equations we can directly compute the level of consumer-demand as well as the capacity of the system for producing investment goods under full employment, viz.

$$C_f = 82,500 \text{ tons}, \quad C_w = 222,000 \text{ tons}, \quad C_t = 550,001 \text{ tons},$$
$$C_b = 5,500 \text{ boats}, \quad I_b = 15,590 \text{ boats}.$$

It is seen first, that approximately 1·3 million acres will be used in wheat production under full employment of labour. However, labour will not be fully employed unless investment demand for boats is 15,590, whereas the demand for private investment is but 2. If the State, for example, were to step in with a loan-financed public works or defence programme of boat-

38

building at the rate of 15,588 p.a., labour will be fully employed and the final solution will appear as in Table 6.

Table 6. *Transactions during twelvemonth*

Output of	Price (wage-unit)	Sold to (wage-unit)					
		1	2	3	4	Con-sumers	State
1. Fishing	0·222	—	—	—	—	18,300	—
2. Wheat	0·111	—	—	—	—	24,500	—
3. Timber	0·011	—	—	—	585	6,110	—
4. Boats	0·309	0·6	—	—	—	1,700	4,809
5. Labour	1·0	16,500	22,000	5,500	5,272	—	—
6. Land	—	—	—	—	—	—	—
7. Interest	—	0·1	—	—	—	—	—
8. Profit	—	1,800	2,500	610	653	—	—
Value produced	—	18,300	24,500	6,110	5,925	—	—

However, failing a State-works programme, there will be unemployment in the boat-building industry and (by virtue of the 'multiplier effect') consequent secondary unemployment in other industries.* Finally, it will be observed that the two food industries here compete for the consumer's pound and any significant technological improvement lowering the price of, say, fish would cause some shift of demand away from wheat.

* This third step in the argument can be carried out as previously—whereas before we assumed total employment to be known and investment demand unknown, the position is now reversed. The new solution can be set out in a transactions table. See also pp. xv and 48.

CHAPTER VI

INVESTMENT
(FOURTH MODEL)

§1. We are familiar with the fact that, in the real world, individuals may choose to allocate their current income partly to current consumption and partly to provision for future consumption. With the introduction of investment goods into the system this further opportunity for choice exists since, by forgoing current consumption, resources can be diverted to producing investment goods which will, in the future, yield consumer-goods.

There is then a demand function for annuities just as there is a demand function for butter. Just as the unit of quantity of butter is the hundredweight, so we shall take as unit of quantity of annuity the sum of £100 to be paid one year from the date of purchase. The price of an annuity is determined by the interest rate (or compensation rate as we shall presently call it), e.g. if the prevailing rate is 5 % p.a., the price of an annuity is £$\frac{100}{1 \cdot 05}$ or £95·24. To the individual spending his current income, annuities are another commodity he can purchase. They commonly take the form of industrial debentures, i.e. fixed-interest securities which are a first charge upon the profits of the industry concerned.*

In sum, the desire to provide for the future produces a demand for annuities while on the other hand the current construction of investment goods is financed by the sale of debentures which, by virtue of the productivity of investment goods, yield a future income or annuity.

§2. The demand function for annuities, as for any other commodity, is determined by individuals' tastes. Given individual tastes and expectations, the demand for annuities will be determined by real income and by relative prices. Should we wish to 'go behind' the behaviourist demand function we may, as in the previous chapter, extend both the equi-marginal utility condition and the budget constraint: the ratio of the marginal utility of a commodity to its price must be the same for all commodities (including annuities); the individual's expenditure equals the sum of the value of his purchases of all commodities (including annuities). The equi-marginal utility condition then

---

* For simplicity we have assumed that there are only one-year redeemable debentures. The argument can readily be extended.

It is assumed that funds to finance investment are obtained through flotation of industrial debentures because we wish to explain the emergence of a rate of compensation which is quoted in the market. If flotation is by share issue or investment in own enterprise, no market rate appears.

40

determines the *ratio* of provision for future consumption in the form of annuities to current consumption of butter, of fish, etc. It is the necessary condition specifying the choice of that ratio which will give maximum satisfaction.

Concerning the form of the demand function there is little we can add to the general argument of the previous chapter. So long as a comparatively small percentage of individual income is spent on annuities, the real income effect will be small and the substitution effect will dominate—with the result that a rise in the compensation rate (a fall in annuity price) will bring about an increased demand for annuities.

§3. The opportunity to provide for future consumption depends (apart from goods-storage and investment-in-self) upon the ability to produce investment goods, i.e. plant and equipment of appreciable life. The construction of investment goods is financed by the sale of debentures—the price of a debenture which yields an annuity of £100 in one year hence being £ $\frac{100}{1+r}$ where r is the rate of compensation (or interest) paid on the debenture.

There is no reason to assume that r must be positive, although the notion that the individual needs to be compensated for the loss of current consumption suggests that this is likely to be so. It is moreover the case that the superior productivity of investment goods may yield a rate of return from which a positive rate of compensation can be paid. The historical appearance of an investment good represents a new method of production, hence an act of innovation. The businessman making the innovation is attracted by the expected *rate of return*—a return which stems from the superior productivity of the new method of production. Consider a simple example: In a community where shore-fishing has prevailed, the invention of boats offers the opportunity for a new method of obtaining fish. The new method will be introduced only if it is more efficient than the old. For if boat-fishing is to be introduced, the community must invest in boats, and since this is only possible if some current consumption is forgone, some compensating future return must be offered. So the new method of production involving the investment good (boats) must be sufficiently efficient to pay a *rate of compensation* for loss of current consumption. Since boat-fishing is usually more productive, this condition is likely to be satisfied and the individual who spends 50 days' labour this year building a boat having a working life of one year will find that next year his fish production exceeds the output of 415 days of shore-fishing—the excess being the 'return' on the investment.

§4. The rate of return on an investment good can be readily computed. Suppose, for example,* that the owner of a fishing fleet knows that an additional

* In this example we shall for simplicity tacitly assume all prices to be constant.

boat costing 79 tons of fish* and having a life of three years will, after making allowance for the cost of the labour which will man the boat,† increase output each year by 30 tons. Now if the rate of return is r, then by definition a current expenditure on boat building of one unit yields $(1+r)$ units at the close of the first year—or, what is the same thing, the yield of 30 units at the end of the first year has a present value of $\dfrac{30}{1+r}$. Further, by definition a current expenditure on boat building of one unit yields $(1+r)^2$ units at the close of the second year—so the present value of the yield of 30 units at the end of the second year is $\dfrac{30}{(1+r)^2}$. Similarly the present value of the third yield of 30 units at the end of the third year is $\dfrac{30}{(1+r)^3}$ after which the working life of the boat is finished. Hence the present value of the boat which is known to be 79 units, equals

$$30\left[\frac{1}{(1+r)}+\frac{1}{(1+r)^2}+\frac{1}{(1+r)^3}\right].$$

From this the rate of return is computed to be 7 %, as the reader can readily satisfy himself by substitution. In equilibrium this rate of return on an increment of investment equals the rate of compensation required to persuade individuals to forgo consumption—for if the marginal rate of return on boat-building exceeds the prevailing rate of compensation it will be profitable for businessmen to bid up the compensation rate and expand investment.

In reality it is precisely such an 'annuity calculation' as this that the businessman must make in deciding whether to expand investment (though because of the uncertainty of receipts in future years he is likely to leave a wide margin for error). But his condition of equilibrium is much more simply stated, viz. that the value of sales must yield normal profit after providing for all ordinary costs, together with both the depreciation charge on capital equipment and the charge of a rate of return on the value of capital equipment equal to the prevailing market compensation rate. If the rate of return on additional investment exceeds the market compensation rate, it is clearly profitable to expand investment.

In passing we may note that in the unusual event of an investment good being both continuously variable and substitutable for other current inputs, then the equi-marginal productivity condition of the firm must be modified since the investment good here yields a series of (one or more) future marginal products. The condition then reads that the ratio of the discounted value of

* I.e. the labour employed in building the boat could alternatively have obtained 79 tons of fish by shore-fishing during the time spent on construction.

† This cost is in fact the output such labour could have produced when engaged in shore-fishing.

the series of marginal products of a factor to the factor's price shall be the same for all factors, i.e.*

$$\frac{\text{Marg. prod. of labour}}{\text{Wage}} = \frac{\text{Marg. prod. of materials}}{\text{Price of materials}} = \cdots$$

$$= \frac{(\text{One year's marg. prod. of boats}).(z)}{\text{Price of boats}},$$

where z must be a figure *less than* the length of life of the boat if the investment is to yield a positive rate of return.† However, if, as is frequently the case, the capital equipment is not substitutable for other inputs, then this complication does not arise for there is no question then of determining the *relative* rates of input of investment goods and other inputs. The overall level of activity of the industry (and so its volume of capital equipment) is, as usual, determined by the condition stated in the preceding paragraph.

§5. The preparedness of the individual to provide for future consumption by carrying out current investment is clearly influenced by the rate of return the investment is capable of producing. He can only be persuaded to buy more debentures if their price is reduced (i.e. the compensation rate raised). On the other hand the businessman is likely to offer more debentures only at a higher price (i.e. he offers a lower compensation rate) because the rate of return per unit of investment is likely to decline as the volume of investment increases, either because of diminishing scale return or substitution in favour of consumer-goods not using the investment good (e.g. a substitution away

---

* For simplicity we assume equal annual returns over the life of the investment. As in the previous statement of the marginal productivity condition, the assumption of constant prices is also temporarily maintained.

† By the 'annuity calculation' we have established that the present value of the series of regular prospective receipts of £T attributable to an investment good over its life of t periods is £$\frac{T(1-R^{-t})}{R-1}$, where R is unity *plus* the rate of return on the investment good (e.g. 5 %) and can be computed if we know the supply price of the investment good.

Now £T is the algebraic product of the marginal productivity of boats (dX_{bf}) and the price of fish (P_f); also for brevity let us write z for $\frac{(1-R^{-t})}{R-1}$.

We may then write the necessary maximum condition in the following form, viz. the price of boats
$$P_b = P_f.dX_{bf}.z, \tag{1}$$
assuming for simplicity that P_f is constant.

Hence $P_f = \frac{P_b}{dX_{bf}.z}$, and by carrying out the same argument for labour and materials we obtain the statement in the text. As to the value of z,
$$z = \sum_{i=0}^{i=t-1} \frac{R^i}{R^i},$$
and since both $R > 1$ and $t > 0$, it follows that z is the sum of t terms each less than unity and so $z < t$. However, the central point is the quite unsophisticated notion that if, in equation (1), z were not less than t, then clearly no return on the investment is possible.

from fish). Equilibrium is reached when the rate of return on investment goods equals the compensation rate, i.e. when the demand for debentures equals their supply.

§6. A further matter may now be introduced. We have implicitly assumed that the entrepreneur has a certain amount of working capital. The size of this is determined by the scale of production, the production function, the period of production and payments habits. Since the entrepreneur may need to borrow the funds and in any event must forgo some alternative use for the capital, we must clearly take account of it in any complete statement of the system. This can be quite simply done by inserting in the cost equation an interest charge on working capital. 'Working capital' may be interpreted broadly to include the value of finished goods which must be kept on hand to meet purchasers' current needs, as well as the value of goods in process and raw materials and the value of liquid funds which must be maintained to run the business.

§7. In the above discussion we have both introduced investment goods and analysed the forces determining their level. Instead of passing on immediately to the next chapter, it is convenient at this point to mention an activity we have so far ignored, namely speculation. Save in somewhat exceptional cases, speculative activity is comparatively unimportant as related to the production of the goods and services which are part of our daily life. But with debentures the position is, potentially at least, rather different. For as a community increases its real wealth by investment, so too is increased the collection of debentures (or rather securities) which are the titles to that wealth. Consider now the possible effect that the existence of such a collection of securities may have on future investment.

Once a particular compensation rate has been established for any time, individuals are apt to regard it as 'normal', i.e. they expect it to continue. For example, suppose the demand for funds by businessmen falls off because of fewer investment opportunities and this results in a fall in the compensation rate in the new issues market, this lower rate will spread to the old debentures whose market price will be bid up; but this rate is below 'normal' and so is expected to rise—or, what is the same thing, the prices of debentures are expected to fall; so the holders of debentures will sell, thereby depressing the price of debentures and raising the compensation rate. So although the proceeds of these sales of debentures will be allocated to current consumption, none the less by maintaining the compensation rate they have succeeded in preventing any possible stimulus to investment which might result from a lower compensation rate.

This then has introduced a speculative demand for debentures, determined by the difference between the expected and existing compensation rates (the expected rate in turn being, for example, an average of rates over some past period). The condition of equilibrium is now that the sum of the ordinary and speculative demands for debentures equals the available stock. If the available stock grows but slowly, it is clear that a large change in speculative demand will significantly affect the rate of compensation and so the terms at which new investment can be undertaken. However, the importance of this excursus into speculative activity should not be overrated—it is probable that speculation can never for very long divert the compensation rate from its long term course as determined by the forces discussed earlier in the chapter.

§8. It is quite a simple matter to develop the original concept of a system of production as set out in Chapter I to include investment activity. For each investment good—whether it be an electric generator or a plough—there is now a new industry to produce it and this industry is described by precisely the same set of relations previously used to describe an industry. For the consumer-good industry using an investment good the set of relations is also as before, but of course the cost equation includes the depreciation and compensation (or interest) charges on the capital equipment (and, as already noted, the equi-marginal productivity condition may be modified). In short, the productive system is formally assembled by setting down for each industry the relations

> The production function;
> The necessary maximum condition;
> The normal profit condition;
> The intersector condition;*
> The cost equation.

In addition, both factor-supply functions and consumer-demand functions are required. So the only new relation introduced (apart from the transactions demand for and the supply of money which are needed to determine the absolute price level) is the demand function for annuities, and of course this demand must in equilibrium be equal to the total supply of annuities (or debentures) from businessmen carrying out investment. However, further discussion of the system as now developed is postponed until all functions of money are introduced in the next chapter.

---

* The simplest form of the intersector condition for an investment goods industry is that the current output of the investment good equals the total quantity of the investment good used in all industries divided by its length of life. As we shall see later the real position is apt to be a little more complex.

CHAPTER VII

MONEY

(FIFTH MODEL)

§ 1. Hitherto we have regarded money as little more than a technical aid to the conduct of the market—though this function is not to be underestimated. It is the purpose of this chapter to point out that money may offer a golden opportunity for hedging—an activity in which people participate because of an amorphous desire to provide against the general possibility of capital loss which may occur if assets are held in non-monetary form. We shall examine the effect of hedging in money upon both the level of investment and the overall level of production.

It has already been pointed out that the efficiency of the market is increased if some commodity is generally accepted in exchange for other commodities. The qualities that a commodity needs in order to be generally accepted are— apart from such physical attributes as homogeneity, divisibility, transport-ability—approximate stability in exchange value at least over a short period. For no one wants to pay a debt with a commodity which he expects to appreciate, nor to accept settlement of a debt with a commodity which will depreciate in value.

However, in organized society there is not merely such a demand for a unit of currency, but also a demand for a commodity which shall serve as 'unit of account', i.e. for a commodity in terms of which other commodities may be measured. It would be a most difficult task for the businessman to ascertain whether a particular line of production will be profitable if he did not have some unit of account in which to express the costs of the factors he needs at various stages of the production process. Clearly the commodity which best fulfils this accounting function is one which most closely approximates stability in value in exchange for other commodities at large. It is not surprising there-fore that the same commodity usually performs both functions of medium of exchange and measure of value, and this commodity we call 'money'.

When a commodity generally accepted as a medium of exchange becomes also used as a measure of value, it is consequently also a standard of value for deferred payments and it (or its physical counterpart which may be merely a slip of paper) may be used as a store of value. The demand for money as a store of value lies in the fact that it yields a 'security return', i.e. if the individual holds his assets in the form of this money commodity he is secure in the knowledge that he can, if necessary, spend his assets immediately, without loss of their capital value—whereas this may not be the case if he holds his assets in wheat or boats or debentures. In short, money is the most liquid of assets. Because of this it offers an excellent opportunity for hedging against the possibility of loss in capital value involved in, say, holding debentures. Holding money as a hedge becomes a further alternative to allocating one's resources to consumption or to holding debentures.

§2. We introduce then a hedging demand function for money. As with other demand functions, it may be derived from a knowledge of tastes. Money for this purpose is another commodity (satisfying the demand for a hedge) and so in order to derive the function the equi-marginal utility condition can be extended to include the ratio of the marginal utility of money to its price (unity). The equi-marginal utility condition determines the choice of ratio in which the individual allocates his command over resources between money, annuities and the several consumer-goods. The budget constraint is likewise extended to include the purchase (or holding) of money. With given tastes and expectations the demand for money is determined by income and by prices—in particular it is likely to be affected by the price of annuities, which varies with the interest rate.

§3. In résumé, money being newly vested with the function of a store of value, we see that the opportunity now exists for monetary saving, i.e. accumulation of the money-commodity. But if the money-commodity has a value which derives wholly (or largely) from the fact of its general acceptability, then accumulation or storing of that commodity, though constituting 'saving' or non-spending, is not in itself provision for the future in any material or social sense, i.e. is not investment. This divorce of the decision to invest from the decision to save is a major characteristic of our monetary society.*

Individuals can increase their inactive holdings of money balances only by reducing their rate of spending either on consumption goods or industrial debentures. So if people increase their hedge in money, the level of effective demand for resources is reduced and the overall level of production of the community will fall.

§4. It is perhaps the outstanding feature of a community where production is highly specialized and each individual's output is produced exclusively for sale in the market, that such a fall in effective demand is 'multiplied' so that the final fall in production is greater. Let us see how this occurs. But before so doing, it may be finally stressed that unless the opportunity existed for hedging in money, a fall in the employment of resources would never occur (save only if society were consciously seeking to conserve exhaustible resources).

The argument should be prefaced by pointing out that the form of the

---

* In all fairness we may note that the decision to abstain from current consumption (i.e. to save) does involve a form of investment in so far as such consumption would have used up exhausting resources such as coal, nickel.

consumer-demand function is such that, above some minimum level of real income, individuals usually save some portion of each additional pound of income. In other words their marginal propensity to consume is less than unity. An immediate implication of this is that full employment of the community's available resources will exist only if, when fully employed, additional expenditures are made which are equal to the volume of savings. Such expenditures may, for example, be on private investment, on public works or on loans to other nations. In the absence of such expenditures the volume of private consumer-demand will be insufficient to purchase the maximum possible output of the community and so in equilibrium some resources will be idle (unless for example the Government were prepared to finance a steady accumulation of stocks).

Now it is clear that a fall, for example, in the rate of investment demand involves a fall in production. Analysing this in more detail, it will be observed that an initial or *primary* decline in the production of investment goods involves a reduction in factor-incomes and so reduced spending on consumer-goods. Unless stocks are to increase indefinitely there must be a fall in production of consumer-goods. But this too will involve a further fall in factor-incomes, a further reduction in consumer-demand and so a further reduction in production of consumer-goods; and so the process continues. However, since people save, they do not reduce their consumer-spending by as much as their incomes, and so these reductions in production of consumer-goods will finally end. The total decline in production of consumer-goods is called the *secondary* fall in production. It can be quite simply shown that if, for example, the marginal propensity to save is constant, the total fall in production (i.e. primary *plus* secondary, as measured by the fall in factor-incomes) equals the primary fall multiplied by the reciprocal of the marginal propensity to save.

From the above discussion we can grasp readily the notion of a *moving equilibrium* of the system of production. Let us suppose for the moment that the demand for investment goods, instead of being constant, in fact fluctuates. This is a wholly reasonable supposition since firms only undertake periodically the task of building a factory or replacing a steam-press. It is easy to see then that the equilibrium level of communal production will rise and fall with the level of such expenditure—reproducing the phenomena of 'boom and depression'. This movement might conceivably be eliminated by compensating changes in, say, government expenditure or even in private consumption demand. However, the moving equilibrium has proved to be an outstanding characteristic of societies where production is almost exclusively for the market and virtually complete specialization the rule.

§5. With the appearance of money as a store of value, debentures now pay a rate of interest, not alone to compensate for loss of current consumption (the 'compensation rate') but also to recompense for the loss of liquidity which results from not holding (i.e. hedging in) money.* We may elaborate this.

Inasmuch as the present value of a commodity differs from its value at a future date it may be said to yield a 'rate of return' (which is not necessarily positive). There are three sources of such a rate of return;† an investment good may yield a positive rate because it is the instrument of a superior method of production; most commodities (e.g. wheat in silo) yield a negative rate because of the costs of the storage which is needed to prevent deterioration;‡ thirdly, a commodity may yield a security return (or liquidity premium) and though perhaps money is in this respect only different in degree rather than in kind from other commodities, it is virtually the sole commodity which has a significant positive security return. The positive rate of return on an investment good will fall if production and use of the good are increased but the rate of return on money is virtually inextinguishably positive—money always gives a security return. Consequently, if an investment is to be undertaken (say in boat-building) the expected rate of return must at least equal the positive rate of interest.§

§6. Now that money is established as a store of value, let us return briefly to the businessman of the previous chapter who is making an innovation involving investment. He needs funds for outlay on the investment good. But because money yields a security return, the expected rate of return on the investment good must be sufficiently high to recompense for loss of liquidity. (We might go further and hazard the comment that, to a point, people are fairly desirous of making some saving under most circumstances—but it really does take a significantly positive interest rate to persuade them not to hold all those savings in money.) Given the need to borrow such funds we have a market rate of interest.

The emergence of the interest rate then has been explained by the need of private businessmen to finance new investment with borrowed funds. This explanation reflects an important characteristic of the capitalist system and our explanation is not substantially affected by the fact that in any event a market rate of interest would probably have emerged because of the

* The rate of interest was previously called the rate of compensation because the second aspect had not then been introduced.

† If the reader feels unfamiliar with this notion, it is best analysed by abstracting all considerations of risk, and then simply considering the exchange in the market of one unit of a commodity to-day for x units in a year's time. If you can get a quote for x which exceeds unity then the 'own rate of return' on the good is positive.

‡ Cigars and spirits are notable exceptions.

§ To compute such a comparison of rates, the own rate of return on each commodity is expressed in terms of a common standard, usually money. This is done by adding (or subtracting) any expected appreciation (or depreciation) of the value of the commodity in terms of the common standard.

nefarious activities of warring and improvident princes (possessing, of course, adequate powers of taxation or nepotism). In the main, a positive interest rate has emerged because businessmen were able to pay it and because owners of funds demanded it because of the loss of both current consumption and liquidity.

Because money always yields a liquidity premium, it seems that there is a minimum below which the interest rate will not fall. For this reason an appreciable drop in the level of investment may not greatly affect the interest rate. Hence the possibility of maintaining the level of activity in the face of a fall in investment through a drop in the interest rate giving a counter-stimulus to consumption or investment, is largely illusory. The funds no longer absorbed by investment will be largely held as inactive balances, and the decline in investment will have a 'multiplier' effect.

§7. There is a speculative demand for money (as for any asset) if people have a specific expectation that other assets will depreciate in terms of it. The importance of speculative demand for assets should not be exaggerated, for it seems probable that speculative activities cannot for long divert the prices of assets from their long-term trend as determined by elements we have already analysed.

None the less it is plain that speculative activity can affect the current prices of assets. For example, an expectation of a fall in the price of debentures will lead to a speculative demand for money and the offer of debentures for sale, thus depressing their price and raising the market rate of interest. The original expectation of a debenture price fall might have developed because the interest rate had fallen, say because of a drop in investment activity, and was consequently expected to return to its previous 'normal'.* Restating the example then, we have a situation where, because a reduced rate of investment causes a reduced offer of new debentures, the interest rate drops below the conception of a normal rate held by some operators who consequently sell securities (and receive savings) thereby limiting the fall in the interest rate. By so doing they limit or prevent a counter-stimulus to the level of investment- and consumption-demand through a drop in the interest rate. However, it would be easy to give undue importance to this effect of speculative activity. It is likely that this type of speculative activity merely succeeds in preventing excessive fluctuations of the interest rate around its long-term trend, which is determined by non-speculative considerations.

§8. We may conclude with a few general comments. At various stages of the argument three kinds of demand for money have been identified: the demand for working balances to carry on the everyday transactions involved

---

* If expectations are determined largely by past experience, the normal or expected interest rate may be regarded as standing in a definite relationship to the average interest rate over some past period—the relation and period being a matter for inquiry.

in producing and distributing the national product; the demand for hedging balances; and the demand for speculative balances. We have considered how, to the person wishing to save for the future, hedging balances are an alternative to holding debentures. The assumption that the sale of industrial debentures is the only method of obtaining funds for investment has been made partly for simplicity, but mainly because this is the most satisfactory way of explaining the emergence of the market interest rate. If funds are obtained by share issue no *market* rate appears—in effect the individual as owner of funds decides the *subjective* rate of interest at which he will provide funds to himself as businessman, since the subscriber to shares is (for good or ill) the owner of the investment goods and potentially at least has some authority in directing their use. The fact that funds *are* obtained by share issue as well as by debenture is in no way inconsistent with our argument—it merely makes the picture a little more complex and realistic. Likewise we have simplified the picture by omitting the possibility of bank finance. Bank finance is in effect finance by debenture (though the debenture may not be marketable) and the only new element introduced is that bank finance is usually associated with a change in the money supply. For the present, however, it is convenient to maintain the assumption that the money supply is fixed, since we are examining equilibrium situations. The behaviour of banks in expanding the money supply belongs more properly to the theory of economic development and as such will be introduced later.

One form only of hedging activity has been introduced in this chapter. Attention should perhaps be drawn to other hedging activities, such as fire and marine insurance, while hedging by diversification of production (or at least by having non-specific plant) may have an importance for industrialists which investigators have failed to appraise. Unfortunately justice cannot be done to such activities in this essay.

Finally, though two new opportunities for economizing activity have been introduced in this and the previous chapter, we have given no 'practical examples' of these two developments culminating in transactions tables for the system of production. Now while such hypothetical examples could be given it is the intention of this essay to give only examples which correspond closely to the kind of empirical investigation which is immediately possible with the type of statistics becoming available in English-speaking countries. And there is good reason to suggest that in the present stage of our knowledge there are special difficulties in determining in practice the equilibrium rate of investment and of the interest rate. For, regarding the former, while we have analysed how the equilibrium volume of capital equipment of the industry may be determined, the somewhat elastic working-life of much equipment gives the entrepreneur considerable freedom in choosing when he shall undertake a given required piece of investment. For this reason there is much to be said for ascertaining directly from the businessman the timing of his planned investments. This questionnaire method is already in use. Later perhaps, when we come to know more of the reasons which determine the timing of a given investment, we shall be able to 'determine' the rate of investment and not simply accept it as a 'datum' supplied by the businessman. As to the interest rate, it will be noted that into the system of relations set out in Chapter VI, §8, we have now introduced a new demand function for money. In fact, we know little of that aspect of individual tastes which determines his hedging activity in money—we should be hard enough put to it to specify a demand for annuities, and still more so a hedging demand function for money. All in all it were wise for the present to take the ruling interest rate also as a datum in our empirical research and let the more ambitious treatment attend upon greater knowledge.

CHAPTER VIII

THE SUPPLY OF FACTORS
(SIXTH MODEL)

§1. Throughout this essay we have assumed knowledge of the factor-supply function of each original resource. This is a perfectly satisfactory procedure. Indeed the factor-supply function (which is a demand function for idle resources), the demand function for a consumer-good, the demand function for annuities, the hedging demand function for money, all have this in common: they are functions describing the behaviour of individuals in the market place, and so it is perfectly logical for us to assert the existence of these functions and then proceed to ascertain them by observation of market activities. But we can also (if we wish) seek to 'go behind' these behaviourist functions in order to 'explain' them. Thus we have previously pointed out that, knowing individuals' tastes, by asserting that they seek to maximize their satisfaction we can derive a demand function for each consumer-good. The same is no less true of the factor-supply function. Each individual is the custodian of some natural resources, even if it be only his own labour-power. His tastes include a desire not only for bread and annuities but also for leisure, i.e. for his own idle labour-power. Since we assert that the individual will so allocate his labour-power between productive activity and leisure as to achieve maximum satisfaction, we can with complete validity extend the argument of Chapter v, §2, to derive also the demand for leisure (the supply of labour) as a function of the price of leisure (the wage-rate) and of the prices of other commodities.* The equi-marginal utility condition is again extended to include the ratio of the marginal utility of leisure to its price (the wage-rate).

§2. The above argument may be extended to the supply of other resources such as land. But as on the whole comparatively little satisfaction is to be gained by the owner of unemployed land (even park-land) it is perhaps probable that the supply of land is likely to be of the most simple form, namely that it is available at any price it can command.

Indeed, in many modern societies the position is not dissimilar with respect to labour. For under their existing institutions a standard working week has been established and individuals have been sufficiently regimented by custom virtually to eliminate the possibility of working less than the current standard. Hence labour tends to be available for the standard working week at any

---

* Instead of assuming that the individual begins with a given income or stocks of commodities ($x_0, y_0, \ldots$) we would now assume that he begins with a given quantity of idle resources. See also E. H. Phelps Brown, *The Framework of the Pricing System*, pp. 146–56.

price it can get. This does not of course necessarily eliminate the possibility that if individuals were asked to work an additional period of say $x \%$ over the standard week they may demand a higher hourly wage-rate (expressed as a percentage of the standard rate) which is determined by their individual tastes. But in fact even this overtime wage-rate has been institutionalized ('time-and-a-half') under trade unionism, and in general the individual employee is left to offer his overtime services at the fixed wage-rate up to the number of hours that he (the employee) is prepared to offer or the employer to demand.

In this matter, then, prevailing institutions are of decisive importance. In countries where modern trade unionism is well established there is little use in seeking to derive the factor-supply functions solely or even partly by reference to individual tastes. This well illustrates the assertion of Chapter II, §2, that individuals may be constrained from maximizing their position by the power of tradition and social institutions. In these circumstances we had best be content with the behaviourist functions.

CHAPTER IX

LOCATION
(SEVENTH MODEL)

§1. Having hitherto tacitly assumed that all production and consumption occur at one place, we shall now recognize that these activities are located in geographic space. It is immediately apparent that the plants producing a commodity will not be evenly spread over the globe. This is because the profitability of production varies with plant location for four reasons: the uneven (relative) distribution of primary factors and their comparative immobility, local variation in transport or transfer costs (of factor and product) owing to the uneven nature of the earth's surface and to other causes, and local variation in tastes and hence in relative consumer-demand for goods; each of these three elements may and does change as between locations so that for the production of any particular commodity some locations are more profitable sites than others; in addition, the existence of 'large-scale' methods of production affects the choice of site because, on this count at least, centralized production will be more profitable than regionally distributed plants.

The course of the ensuing analysis may here be reviewed. In §2 there is a discussion of the determinants of location which is designed to elaborate the statements of the preceding paragraph. Then in §3 it is argued that an explanation of the location of production can be built up by the following procedure. The globe is conceived as divided into localities and these in turn are grouped into regions. A locality is defined by the fact that it has only one market point (which is also a consuming point) at which all output of the locality is sold. A region is a group of localities defined by the fact that original factors are perfectly mobile within the region and perfectly immobile as between regions. The theory is then constructed by considering first the determination of location in a closed locality, then in a closed region, and finally in a globe or closed group of regions.

These two sections may prove not a little tedious to the reader who is mainly interested in results and he may prefer to proceed directly to the application of the theory in §4. There, having assumed for simplicity that the locality and the region are identical, we point out that the so-called 'principle of comparative cost advantage' is a necessary condition* which businessmen must satisfy if they are to choose locations of maximum profit, and we then proceed to determine the level of production of commodities in each region.

---

* I.e. businessmen will produce in any region those commodities in which its comparative advantage is greatest (or its comparative disadvantage least).

§2.* Consider the elements which cause a firm's profit to differ in various locations and which thereby determine the location of production.† As we are here seeking merely to ascertain and examine the mode of operation of the determinants, the following assumption may conveniently be made: The entrepreneur setting up his plant plans to produce a particular level of output and to sell a definite percentage of this at each of certain specified market points. That is, the firm plans the total and geographical allocation of its output. In these circumstances it follows that, maximum profit being the aim, the location chosen for the production unit will be the minimum total cost location for the planned output. The cost of production, including the cost of obtaining materials and of marketing the product, will vary in different locations in a manner determined by: transfer-costs for material goods (raw, processed and finished) as determined by both the transportability of various goods and by the local variation in transport resources and facilities; the size of the industry and the method of production; location of markets for outputs; location of sources of inputs. This fourth item, however, is heterogeneous and comprises five operative elements: location of original material factors; existence of several vertical stages in production; transfer-costs of labour and investible funds; non-specificity of factors; substitutability of factors. The remainder of this section is devoted to a review of the operation of these eight distinguishable sources of cost variation as between alternative locations.

For the moment we shall assume that the location of markets and of original material factors are given and on this basis shall proceed to examine the determination of transfer-costs at alternative locations. For simplicity we also begin with the assumptions (successively discarded) that there are no economies of size or concentration, only two vertical stages in production, zero transfer-costs of labour and investible funds, only one use for each material factor and no substitutability between factors.

The determinants of transfer-costs of material goods include, of course, the determinants of the demand for and supply of transport service and so of its price. But the determinants which cause transfer-costs—from raw material source to final consumer—to vary at different production-locations are originally, i.e. before the development of such transport facilities as roads and railways, as follows:

(1) The weight-losing (and bulk-losing) in process quality of materials, thus affecting the relative transfer-costs of input and output.

(2) Multiple-loading costs—for it is possible to reduce loading and unloading costs by, for example, locating at a raw material or market centre.

* The reader may choose to pass this section and the next and to proceed direct to §4.
† This section draws heavily upon the work of B. Ohlin, *Interregional and International Trade*.

(3) Distance from market, for this may affect: transport costs; the quality of goods, because of handling or the time required for transport; the extent, immediacy or intimacy of producers' knowledge of changes in market conditions.

(4) Non-uniformity of geographical features *ex visu* transport: proximity to water transport and natural harbours; proximity to flat rather than mountainous terrain; climate, costs of transfer being in general less, the more equable the climate.

(5) 'Artificial' factors—differential taxation and subsidy; risks of piracy.

(6) Different language, customs and law, resulting in ignorance and risk.

(7) Concentration of related firms. For example, subsidiary enterprise supplying materials or accessories to another firm reduces transfer-costs through small distance and intimate contact.

These primary determinants of transfer-cost variation determine in part the location of industry, whose appearance and growth in turn may result in the development of a transport industry whose location is determined also by the foregoing elements, but, in particular, by the existing location of factors which is interpreted to include the location of production and to include the sources of power for transport facilities, by topography and climate, and by differential taxation or subsidy.

The development of the transport industry in turn determines the location of production also because transfer-costs are affected by:

(8) Non-uniformity of geographical facilities: points where transport facilities converge or touch have better transport relations (and with a wider area) and so have lower transfer-costs; a break in transport facilities, as at a port, tends to cause production to be located there in order to avoid extra costs of loading and unloading; the greater the regularity of traffic, the less the delay in transit and so the less the transfer-cost.

(9) Differential pricing policies of transport companies.

Reviewing these determinants of transfer-cost, it is seen that for any given combination of markets for output, we may determine the minimum transfer-cost location relative to each possible combination of raw material sources. The lowest of the minimum transfer-cost points will be chosen and the sources of raw material giving such a point will be the sources used. In this way the location of both primary and secondary industry is determined.

However, transfer-costs do not alone determine location. The remaining determinants may now be successively introduced. Technical economies of scale or concentration may offset the higher transfer-costs which could otherwise only be avoided by decentralization. The non-divisibility of certain factors, the continuous nature of the processes to which a material is submitted (e.g. hot metals), the avoidance of waste (e.g. the use of hot gases), are agglomerating tendencies in the location of production.

That the location of the consumers' market is a determinant of the location of productive activity is clear. The problem here is what determines the size, character and location of consumers' markets. For the present the location of all factors is still assumed given. Suppose further that the conditions of ownership are known (e.g. that the factors in a district are owned by the residents who own no other factors). Suppose thirdly that tastes are known. From these elements the location, size and character of consumer-demand and hence of consumers' markets are determined. However, in reality there is a relation of interdependence here: while the location of consumers' markets determines the location of industry, the latter—inasmuch as it is determined by other elements, especially resource location—is a determinant of the local distribution of factors, not least of labour, and hence of the location of consumers' markets.

The geographical distribution of original material factors is a fundamental determinant of location of industry. Goods of the 'first order'—raw materials and crude food—must be produced where natural resources are sufficient in quantity and quality; and these locations will be adopted if transfer relations to other co-operating factors and to final markets are adequate. The location of production of goods of 'higher order' is determined, *inter alia*, by transfer-costs as already argued.

It is now recognized that the vertical structure of production may contain more than two stages. The place where process materials are manufactured is at the same time a producing point, a 'raw material' source and a market for the product of the preceding stage. Each stage acts as a market for the preceding one. The location of the several successive processing units is clearly interdependent. 'Given a certain distribution of raw material sources and markets, the localization of the later stages of production is governed by the relative transportability of the different sorts of commodities.'*

Hitherto it has been assumed that costs of transfer of labour and investible funds are zero. But recognizing now that such transfer-costs are positive, it is seen that the local distribution of productive factors is affected and hence the location of productive activity. On this B. Ohlin concludes that the 'actual distribution of [productive factors] at any given moment is a function of (1) localization at earlier times, (2) changes in domestic supply through births, savings, etc., and (3) interlocal movements which the local price differences are able to effect in spite of the incomplete mobility of labour and capital. And the prices and price differences at any one moment are governed by the mutual interdependence price system, in which all the various elements operate together.'

* B. Ohlin, *op. cit.* p. 190.

'Evidently no simple explanation or description of the local distribution of mobile factors is possible, as would be so if their mobility were such as to equalize their nominal prices. In that case the system of relations which governs prices would also govern their distribution. As it is, a concrete description of the actual distribution of labour and capital assumes an investigation into the circumstances behind elements (2) and (3).'*

The discussion of the determinants of location is completed with the reintroduction of the two forms of economizing activity which depend respectively on the existence of non-specificity and substitutability of factors. Of non-specificity all that need be said here is that the type of manufacture which is able to pay the highest price for a factor, obtains control over it—and in this way is determined the location of each form of productive activity. Of substitutability we may point out first, the possibility of varying the ratio of factors employed is now recognized so that it is immediately seen that the transfer-cost of any such factor is an element determining that ratio, and secondly, the existence of resources of different quality can now be introduced, and this—though it may run counter to such other determinants as transfer-cost—is seen to be a distinct determinant of location.

§3.† The problem is now to specify a method of analysing the determination of the level of production of each commodity in each locality. Consider first a closed locality having a single market where all output is sold. To solve this problem we require the fact that an 'industry' is specified, not alone by its product but also by its method of production, i.e. its production function. The production functions for a commodity may differ because of the different processes involved, because different factors are employed (e.g. land of lower fertility), or because distance of plant from the market requires a greater input of transport factors.

We postulate that there is a finite number of production functions for any commodity. These functions are distinguished according to each of the criteria just stated. With regard to the spatial criterion, rather than use geographical co-ordinates we may use a grid (whether square or concentric) to divide the locality into numbered areas or sites. The analysis may then be made as accurate as we choose merely by increasing the fineness of the grid. Having constructed the argument in this wise, we are then able to determine which 'methods of production' will be used—and hence how much of each commodity will be produced at each location. (It is formally immaterial whether each industry provides its own transport to market or uses the services of a transport industry.) It can be seen intuitively that this problem is soluble, for the location of production will be the result of a 'balancing' of varying advantages, such as fertility, depth of mineral deposits, distance from market, availability of cheap water transport and so forth.

* *Op. cit.* pp. 225–6. † The reader may choose to proceed directly to §4.

However, for the moment let us proceed to the second stage of our construction and consider a region or closed group of localities (each locality having its own market point at which all its produce is sold)—the group being specified by the fact that primary factors are perfectly mobile within the group* (and, as we shall see later, perfectly immobile across group boundaries). The problem is now to show that the location of industry in the group is determinate. Now it is clear that transfer-costs from one market point to another are determinate, and for simplicity in presentation we may take these to be parameters. Further, a condition of equilibrium is that the price of a commodity at different market points shall vary by its transfer-cost.

To develop the argument, a notation is used whereby each commodity produced in a locality (or 'area') is distinguished from every other commodity produced in that and other localities. For example, there is no commodity 'wheat', but a number of commodities 'area 1 wheat', 'area 2 wheat', and so on. The effect of this convention is that no commodity so defined is both produced in and imported into a locality. This somewhat tedious device is initially necessary in order to determine which localities will produce and will export which commodities. Without it, there is no way of initially deciding what sign to give to transfer-costs on commodities.†

A numeral superscript is affixed to all quantities and prices to specify the relevant locality of production (for quantities of input and output) and of market (for price of output) respectively. This of course does not apply to the price of original factors which are uniform throughout the region. It is assumed that the prices of factors employed in a locality accrue as incomes to residents and where this is not so, appropriate adjustment must be made. The consumption of residents is similarly specified by a numeral superscript. The location of production is then determinate—the siting of each industry in each locality being ruled by the condition that the price of a commodity at different market points varies only by its transfer-cost. It may be pointed out that with this second stage of the model, we are also now able to take account of the possibility of a choice between having one large-scale plant in a single locality as against having smaller plants, one in each locality.

The third stage of the construction involves the determination of production in a closed system comprising a number of regions—the regions being specified by the fact that factors are completely immobile across regional boundaries. In this connexion it may be pointed out that mobility of primary factors is a substitute for mobility of final commodities. For this reason it is necessary that the character of the mobility of factors be known before the location of

---

* Since it is the proportions in which factors are combined which are significant, one factor can always be immobile.

† The convention implies that in determining the system, we construct sets of relations for industries which will never in fact exist unless subsidized.

industry (and hence the character of interregional trade) may be determined. The model carried to this third level is again determinate. For, in respect of each region, we set out as before the relations determining both location in the localities and in the region; and then, using yet another number system to specify regions, they are linked by the requirement that the price of a commodity at one market point in a region shall differ from its price at one market point in each other region by a transfer-cost parameter. Each region has of course its own factor supply functions.

It will be observed that the virtue of having constructed the argument at three levels is that we are able to consider, in some degree separately, the four determinants of location: transfer-costs; consumer-demand, and also lumpy factors; the relative distribution of resources.

Throughout the rest of this essay we shall employ the assumption that the locality and the region are identical. This action can only be justified as a temporary expedient designed to prevent our exposition becoming excessively complex. Henceforth then, there is assumed to be but one market point in each region.

§4. The determination of the location of industry is readily separable into two problems: the first is to ascertain which regions will produce which commodities; the second, to ascertain the level of output of each commodity produced in each region. The solution to the first is given in principle by the condition that the commodities produced in any region shall be those in which its comparative advantage is greatest (or its comparative disadvantage least), i.e. even if Queensland is more efficient in producing all commodities than Victoria, Queensland will not produce all commodities itself but will specialize on those in which its technical superiority *relatively* to Victoria is greatest and will obtain its other requirements by trade with Victoria, who will concentrate on producing those commodities in which its technical inferiority is least. This 'principle of comparative cost advantage' is illustrated in an example below.* However, if there are diminishing scale returns in the production of a commodity in a region which began production with a comparative advantage, we may find that after world demand reaches a certain level, plants can also be set up in other regions. The principle of comparative cost advantage as a guide to regional specialization also tacitly assumes that each region specializing in a commodity is sufficiently large to meet all requirements of other regions (and of course if it is not, then infinitely diminishing scale returns are abruptly reached at the limit of regional resources). Finally, we may point out that greater technical efficiency† is but one reason for

* See also D. Ricardo, *Principles of Political Economy* (1817), ch. 7. ('Everyman' edition, 1917, p. 82.)

† 'Technical efficiency' must itself be carefully interpreted for it may result from climate or from managerial efficiency as readily as from say more zealous labour or more fertile soil.

a region having a comparative cost advantage in the production of a commodity. For example, if the ratio of population to land is much lower in Victoria than in Queensland, then on this account land will be the cheaper (relatively to labour) in Victoria and so this region will have a comparative cost advantage in the production of such commodities as wool where land is a major input in production. In reality there is usually little difficulty in knowing in which regions commodities will be produced* and so we may now proceed immediately to the second problem.

To illustrate the determination of the level of regional output, a simple example may be taken of two regions capable of producing three commodities —the number of regions and goods can be readily increased when the method of solution is established. Since by definition each region is an entity with a given group of resources, each region will have its own factor-supply-, production- and consumption-functions for each industry. The sole new relation that is introduced into the discussion is the requirement that the price of a commodity shall not vary as between regions by more than its transfer-costs. To bring out the argument most clearly we shall assume constant scale returns and that whereas the first region, Queensland, is more efficient than the second region, Victoria, in the production of both the commodities sugar and wheat, it is comparatively much more efficient in the production of sugar. Transport costs being a minor element in the costs of production, we find that Queensland will produce sugar and will leave wheat production entirely to the less efficient Victoria (assuming tacitly that Victoria is big enough to be able to satisfy Queensland's demand for wheat—and conversely with regard to sugar). It is convenient to assume the transport industry to be owned by Victorians shipping wheat to Queensland and returning with sugar. Each region also has a fishing industry, for because of the perishability of the product no interregional trade in fish is practicable. The institutional data are then as follows:

QUEENSLAND

Factor-supply functions

The work force of 10,000 men is available at any price it can obtain.

Production functions

Sugar. The intake of labour is 0·5 man-year per ton.
(Wheat. The intake of labour is 0·1 man-year per ton.)
Fish. The intake of labour is 0·6 man-year per ton.

Normal profit

In each industry this is 6 % of the value of output.

---

* It is as well this is the case—otherwise it would be necessary to follow the tortuous iterative procedure of trying each possibility.

Consumption functions

These are here set out in a simple form showing *expenditure* on each good as determined by income and by the price of each good (expenditure, income and prices being each measured in wage-units):

$$C_w P_w = 0.3\,Y - 48{,}000\,P_w + 300\,P_f,$$
$$C_s P_s = 0.15\,Y,$$
$$C_f P_f = 0.55\,Y + 48{,}000\,P_w - 300\,P_f,$$

where Y (the regional income) is $\dfrac{1}{0.94}\cdot$(wage bill).*

VICTORIA

Factor-supply functions

The work force of 11,000 men is available at any price it can obtain.

Production functions

Wheat. The intake of labour is 0·15 man-year per ton.
(Sugar. The intake of labour is 2·0 man-years per ton.)
Fish. The intake of labour is 0·6 man-year per ton.
Transport. The intake of labour is 0·0001 man-year per ton-mile.†

Normal profit

In each industry this is 6 % of the value of output.

Consumption functions

$$C_w P_w = 0.3\,Y,$$
$$C_s P_s = 0.2\,Y - 1160\,P_s + 200\,P_f,$$
$$C_f P_f = 0.5\,Y + 1160\,P_s - 200\,P_f$$

(all prices and quantities here being Victorian, i.e. more accurately,

$$^{V}C_w\cdot{}^{V}P_w = 0.3\,{}^{V}Y, \text{ etc.}).$$

Finally, the distance between the two regions is given as 200 miles.

It is clear from the consumer-demand functions that people will demand all that can be produced and hence there will be full employment. However, because of its immobility, labour will have a different price in the two regions. For convenience we shall use the Queensland wage-rate as unit of account in terms of which all other prices are expressed. The method of solution is then as follows. First, from the cost equations and from the condition that prices of a commodity shall vary as between regions only by its transfer (or transport) cost, we may write down all commodity prices in terms of the

* The consumption function for wheat is such that imported wheat is competitive with home-produced fish and imported wheat will be demanded only if it can be purchased at a price lower than the home cost of producing wheat.
† For simplicity we have been assuming direct labour to be the sole input which must be paid for. In reality, of course, even if land were free there would, say in the transport industry, at least be indirect labour costs in the cutting of timber and building of boats.

wage-rates (one of which is unity). Second, by substituting these prices in the consumption functions, we may write down all consumer-demands in terms of the wage-rates. Third, from the institutional data we know that in equilibrium the value of Queensland's purchases from Victoria equal the value of Victoria's purchases from Queensland $({}^QC_w . {}^QP_w = {}^VC_s . {}^QP_s)$.* We may immediately substitute in this the prices and quantities already obtained and we obtain the result that, the Queensland wage-unit being numéraire, the Victorian wage-rate is 0·3596 wage-units. Fourthly, we are now able to write down for each region all outputs save the one which we leave to be determined by the overall requirements which limit total production by the available resources. That is we determine ${}^VC_s$ and ${}^QC_s$ by the previous steps and then from

$$0·5({}^QC_s + {}^VC_s) + 0·6{}^QC_f = 10,000 \text{ (man-years)}$$

we determine ${}^QC_f$. Similarly, having determined ${}^VC_w$ and ${}^QC_w$ from the previous steps we can obtain ${}^VC_f$ from

$$0·15({}^QC_w + {}^VC_w) + 0·6{}^VC_f + 0·02({}^QC_w + {}^VC_s) = 11,000 \text{ (man-years)}.$$

The final results can once again be set down in a transactions table (Table 7).

The advantage gained from regional specialization is apparent merely from examining the equilibrium prices: Queensland is obtaining wheat for about one-ninth of the price of sugar, whereas she could produce it only for one-fifth of the price of sugar; Victoria is obtaining sugar for about 9 times the price of wheat, whereas she could produce it only for about 13 times the price of wheat. The advantage may be shown in another way (Fig. 12): Queensland's sugar production is 3484·9 tons (including home consumption of 3000 tons) involving a labour force of 1742 men. In the absence of trade this labour force could produce 3484 tons of sugar or 17,420 tons of wheat or any combination of sugar and wheat on line *AB*. But under trade Queensland is consuming 3000 tons of sugar and 4018·6 tons of wheat, i.e. she is at point *C*, a real income which is quite beyond her production potential save under trade—even though she is most efficient in producing both sugar and wheat.

---

* Read ${}^QC_w$ = Queensland's consumption of wheat;
                       ${}^QP_w$ = Queensland's price of wheat.

This result is obtained as follows. Consider the overall activity of Queensland. We know:

Value of Q's production	= Q's factor incomes [from the cost equations].
Q's factor-incomes	= Q's consumption expenditure [from the consumption functions]
	= Q's consumption expenditure on (home-produced goods *plus* imports).
But value of Q's production	= Q's consumption expenditure on home-produced goods *plus*
	V's consumption expenditure on Q's goods [from the intersector conditions].
Hence Q's consumption expenditure on imports	= V's consumption expenditure on Q's goods.

Table 7(a). *Queensland*

Output of	Price (wage-unit)	Sold to (wage-units)			
		1	2	Victoria	Consumers
1. Sugar	0·532	—	—	260	1596
2. Fish	0·638	—	—	—	8770
3. Victorian wheat	0·065	—	—	—	260
4. Labour	1·0	1743	8258	—	—
5. Profit	—	113	512	—	—
Value produced	—	1856	8770	—	—

Table 7(b). *Victoria*

Output of	Price (wage-unit)	Sold to (wage-units)				
		1	2	3	Queensland	Consumers
1. Wheat	0·0574	—	—	—	231	1260
2. Fish	0·2294	—	—	—	—	2680
3. Transport	0·0075	—	—	—	29	4
4. Queensland sugar	0·532*	—	—	—	—	260
5. Labour	0·3596	1402	2520	32	—	—
6. Profit	—	89	160	1	—	—
Value produced	—	1491	2680	33	—	—

* The price to Victorian shippers f.o.b.

§5. In the argument of §4 prices are measured in terms of the Queensland wage-rate solely in order to avoid unnecessary detail. Recognizing that prices are usually expressed in terms of money, we may see the more readily how it is that the wage-rates are different in the two regions: if the Queensland and Victorian wage-rates were the same, all Queensland prices would be lower than Victorian, so Victorians would transfer their spending from Victorian goods to Queensland, thereby forcing up the Queensland prices and wage-rate relatively to the Victorian. This process will only reach equilibrium when the Victorian wage-rate and so Victorian prices have become sufficiently low to attract a Queensland demand for Victorian goods equal to the Victorian demand for Queensland goods.

If for the purpose of exposition we may once again indulge in the assumption that the sole demand for money is to carry out the transactions incident to producing and distributing the social product, let it be given that this transactions demand for money (by the populace of both regions since they have a common currency)

$$M_{TO} = 0.235 \times \text{(Value of total production of both regions)}$$

and that the supply of money from the banking system is £3,488,900. Then it is readily found that the Queensland wage-rate is £1000 p.a. and we may now express all other prices in £. Apart from enabling us to express prices in £, this explicit introduction of a transactions demand for money leaves the argument and results of §4 unaffected.

QUEENSLAND

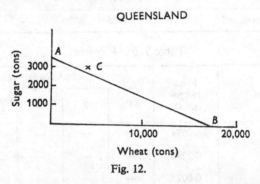

Fig. 12.

§6. Proceeding a step further, let us now suppose that Queensland has one currency (pounds) and Victoria another (crowns), neither of course being accepted outside its 'home' region. Then there is a new price introduced—the 'rate of exchange' or price of pounds in terms of crowns. Still assuming that the sole demand for money is to carry on transactions, if we have the data

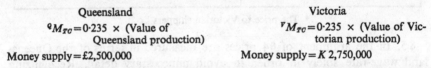

Queensland	Victoria
$^Q M_{TO} = 0.235 \times$ (Value of Queensland production)	$^V M_{TO} = 0.235 \times$ (Value of Victorian production)
Money supply = £2,500,000	Money supply = K 2,750,000

then it is readily seen that the wage-rate in Queensland is £1000 p.a. and that in Victoria it is K 1000 p.a. This being the case the reader will rightly guess that the equilibrium exchange rate is £0.3596 to the crown—or roughly three crowns to the pound.* Apart from enabling us to express the prices in each region in terms of its own currency and to state the exchange rate, the intro-

* This may be confirmed by reworking the balance of payments equation: Queensland's imports equal her exports when valued *in a common currency*. (The condition that prices vary between regions by their transfer-costs also assumes that the prices are expressed *in a common currency*.)

duction of a second currency leaves the argument and results of §4 unaffected. In short, the mere division of a single currency area into regions each having their own currency leaves all equilibrium levels of output, input and relative prices (expressed in a common currency) quite unchanged.

However, division of a single currency area into several regions, does admit of a change in the method of reaching equilibrium. First be it said that the real significance of the exchange rate is that it provides an escalator whereby the entire structure of factor-prices in one region can be scaled up or down by comparison with the structure of factor-prices in another region (or regions). For example, a fall in demand for Victorian exports gives her an excess of imports over exports and to rectify this her crown may be depreciated over-night vis-à-vis the £, thus scaling down Victorian factor-prices and making her goods more attractive on a price basis to Queensland. Now if the two regions have a single currency (or, what is the same thing, if the exchange rate were *fixed*)* some other mechanism must perforce be used to scale down Victorian factor-prices and so eliminate the excess of imports. There are two such alternatives. The first is an authoritarian overall cut in all Victorian money incomes—a device which is seldom used because of both political and administrative difficulties.† The second is a gradual piecemeal reduction in Victorian factor-prices by the firms employing them. This readjustment of the Victorian price level by changing internal prices instead of the external price (i.e. the exchange rate) is apt to be rather slow and to that extent a change in the exchange rate is a more efficient method of reaching equilibrium.‡ Both methods, of course, may involve some transitional unemployment during the readjustment.§

As regards the level of the exchange rate, mention should perhaps be made here of the 'purchasing power parity theory' which avers that the exchange

---

* A single currency and a fixed exchange rate come to the same thing so long as the central banking authority is not carrying out 'monetary management' (i.e. insulation or sterilization of changes in the money supply by open-market operations or other methods). Cf. League of Nations, *International Currency Experience*.

† Cf. Australian experience in 1931 in cutting money wage-rates.

‡ If the supply of factors is highly sensitive to internal money factor-prices but insensitive to exchange-rate changes (a variant of Keynes's money illusion) then exchange-rate variation will give a different (higher employment) equilibrium. But this is unlikely to be important save as a short-run effect.

§ Under the gold bullion standard, whenever there was an excess of imports an outflow of gold resulted which then caused the banking system to cut down the level of internal real investment, thereby forcing down internal factor-prices before gold stocks were exhausted. This mechanism of bringing down the price level necessarily also resulted in appreciable unemployment which would be absent under a variable exchange-rate system.

Some of the by-products of the readjustment process may be important. For example, in a time of rising foreign demand for wool, the sheep farmer makes a windfall gain during the adjustment period if the exchange rate is fixed, but not if it varies. For his purchasing power is raised immediately while that of the rest of the community rises gradually during the period.

rate between two regions' currencies equals the ratio of their internal price levels (so that, for example, if the home price level doubles, then twice as much home currency must be given to obtain a unit of foreign currency). This theory presumably stems from the condition that the price of an interregionally traded commodity is the same in each region when expressed in a common currency and after making allowance for transfer-costs, e.g.

$$^\varrho P_s = {}^v P_s . \frac{R_£}{K} - {}^v P_t . \frac{R_£}{K}$$

where $^v P_t$ is the Victorian price of transport (in crowns) per ton of sugar and $\frac{R_£}{K}$ is the exchange rate (0·3596). Hence

$$\frac{^\varrho P_s}{^v P_s} + t = \frac{R_£}{K},$$

where t is the transport charge per crownsworth of sugar. Since we can state such an equation for any interregionally traded good and since the t's will tend to cancel (being positive on exports and negative on imports), it is clearly meaningful to suggest that the rate of exchange equals the ratio of the internal price levels of interregionally traded goods. However, we cannot proceed from this to postulate the purchasing power parity theory if only because many goods are rarely interregionally traded whether because of their perishability (fresh foods), or their intrinsic nature (personal services). Since the prices of non-interregionally traded goods may not keep in step with the movement of prices of traded goods, the theory oversimplifies the picture and does not offer a short-cut method of computing the equilibrium level of the exchange rate.

§7. In determining the location of industry and the level of production in each region, we have at the same time determined the course of trade—the quantity of each commodity demanded by each region of each other region. As regards the balance of trade (or more correctly the balance of current payments), we know of any region (say, Victoria) that

Vic. regional income = value of Vic. regional production;*
= Vic. expenditure on own goods + value of exports.†

Further, since

Vic. regional income = Vic. expenditure on own goods + value of imports + increase in money holdings;‡

it follows that the balance of trade

Value of exports − Value of imports = increase in money holdings.

An excess of exports over imports can occur, of course, only if loans are made

---

* From cost equations.   † From intersector conditions.
‡ This is an identity defining 'increase in money holdings'.

to or assets* acquired from foreign regions to an amount matching the increase in monetary holdings, while the converse also holds.

As we have seen, trade between regions arises because *relative* commodity prices are different in the regions. This will be the case if differences in the relative availability of factors or in the production functions or entry conditions are not balanced by one another or by differences in demand conditions (such for example, that in the region where commodity *a* can be produced relatively cheaply, there is an equally greater preference for *a*). Lumpiness of factors is a second cause of interregional trade—for the possibility of using such factors depends on the extent of the market and hence on the possibility of trade. The transfer-costs of commodities clearly limit the extent of trade. However, in so far as trade is possible, it is accompanied by an interregional equation of commodity prices and a movement towards an increase in the overall volume of production because of regional specialization.

The reader will have observed that in introducing separate currencies in §6, we transformed our regions into 'nations' and since then the analysis has been of international trade. Special interest attaches to the determination of location with respect to national regions not only because factors are often especially immobile between such regions, but also because governments alter commodity transfer-costs at will by tax, subsidy and prohibition. In addition, the formation of a currency area permits a nation to indulge in 'monetary management' so that, given a sufficient supply of international assets or credulous lenders, it can determine its levels of production to a large degree independently of the outside world. It can, for example, if confronted by a fall in demand for its exports, maintain home employment, production and prices by a bank-financed programme of public works or private investment—and this, without altering its exchange rate, at least so long as its gold and foreign currency reserves hold out to finance the deficit in its balance of trade. But this introduces into the productive system a new pattern of collective action, discussion of which we must postpone.

* Including bonds, equities, monetary gold, overseas currencies.

CHAPTER X

ALTERNATIVE METHODS OF PRODUCTION
(EIGHTH MODEL)

Hitherto the existence of alternative methods of producing a commodity has been virtually ignored. Wherever such alternatives exist, one method may be chosen to the exclusion of others because of its low cost of production or, if diminishing returns to scale prevail, several methods of production may all be used if demand is sufficiently extensive. To clarify ideas, two points should be noted. First, an 'industry' is defined not only by its product but also by its method of production: if, for example, Bessemer converters and open-hearth furnaces are capable of producing identical steels, we have not one steel industry but two, the Bessemer-steel and the open-hearth steel industries. Second, the methods of producing a commodity (as recorded by their production functions) are different not only if different processes are involved but also if different factors are employed (e.g. even if lands of different fertility are used) or because distance from market requires a greater input of transport factors. We have already recognized that variations in location may involve differences in production functions (we distinguished, for example, the Queensland sugar industry and the Victorian sugar industry). It must now also be recognized that if wheat is produced on land of three different fertilities, then there are three wheat industries.*

There is no need to enter into further discussion of alternative methods of production, for the choice of method is made by the businessman by the quite pedestrian method of working out the costs of production involved in each case. After all, it is clear enough that as between two methods of production, if one is consistently cheaper then it alone will be used, but if that initially cheaper method is subject to diminishing scale returns or is limited by scarcity of specific factors, then at some stage the other method may also be brought into productive operation.†

* There is no escaping this. Only in a few special cases can we simplify the argument by applying a conversion factor to reduce different lands to a common denominator having the same price.

† The procedure involves the same two steps as were followed in Chapter IX. First, we must ascertain which methods will be used; second, what the levels of output of each will be (again using an equi-price condition).

CHAPTER XI

INTRA-INDUSTRY FACTOR ALLOCATION
(NINTH MODEL)

§1. Hitherto we have assumed that the output any industry obtains from a given group of resources is the same irrespective of the number of firms into which the industry is divided. It is possible that this is not the case. It might be that the board of management of a firm can only cope easily with a given volume of factors and beyond this critical level the efficiency of managerial co-ordination declines. If this were the case then a new opportunity for economizing activity appears, namely that of the most efficient allocation of factors between the several firms producing the industry's output. For if the industry is to produce maximum output from a given group of factors, then the firm with greater capacity for managerial co-ordination must produce more than others. The present chapter analyses this development and the discussion has the incidental advantage that it explicitly brings into the picture the firm—which is after all the ultimate unit in which decisions to produce are made.

Putting this new problem in another way: the question is, given the aggregate volume of sales of the industry, how are these sales allocated between member firms? What are the *relative* levels of activity of the member firms?

§2. Let us take it that the firm is unable to affect the prices of the factors it employs. Then the necessary condition that the firm must satisfy if it is to make maximum profit is:

The price of each variable input shall equal its marginal revenue product.*

Since, as more of the factor is employed, the marginal revenue product of a factor will ultimately decline (whether because it is a successively poorer substitute for other inputs, because of diminishing scale returns or because consumers will only buy more of the product at a lower price), it follows that if the price of the factor is less than its marginal revenue product then the firm can increase profits by expanding output; and if the price of the factor exceeds its marginal revenue product the firm can increase profits by contracting output.

---

* The marginal revenue product of a factor is defined as the increase in total sales revenue which results from selling the product obtained by employing an additional unit of the factor. If we measure the input of the factor in a sufficiently small unit, the marginal revenue product is numerically equal to the marginal revenue productivity of the factor which is the rate of change of total sales revenue with respect to the input of the factor.

It is convenient to restate this necessary maximum condition in an equivalent form (in two parts) as follows:

(i) The price of the nth variable input shall equal its marginal revenue product;

(ii) The ratio of the marginal product of a factor to its price shall be the same for *all* variable factors (including the nth factor).

The second of these is the familiar equi-marginal productivity condition determining the relative rates of input of all variable factors. The first determines the most profitable scale of output of the firm. Since each firm has such a scale condition it follows that the scale conditions determine the relative outputs of all member firms in the industry.

The information required to determine the most profitable scale of operations of the firm is clearly somewhat difficult to obtain, for to ascertain the marginal revenue product of a factor the firm needs not only technical data but also information about consumers' tastes and demands and about the behaviour of actual and potential competitors. Even in the simplest case where, though diminishing managerial efficiency causes diminishing scale returns, all firms in the industry are similar in managerial capacity and are identical in size, this problem of information persists. For example, the marginal revenue product of a factor is always equal to the algebraic product of the value of its marginal product and an algebraic factor which is the sum of unity and the reciprocal of the relevant price elasticity of demand (ϵ) for the firm's product. Hence the scale condition can be set down as

$$P_n = vmp_n \cdot \left(1 + \frac{1}{\epsilon}\right).$$

Under the similarity assumption just introduced, the output of the industry equals the output of the firm multiplied by the number of firms in the industry. From this it immediately follows that ϵ, the price elasticity of demand for the firm's output, equals the price elasticity of demand for the industry's output (E) *minus* the elasticity (μ) of the number of firms in the industry in response to a change in the price of the product,* i.e.

$$\epsilon = E - \mu.$$

Even if E can be readily ascertained, the value of μ is difficult to know and hence it is difficult for the firm to use the scale condition in any accurate way. The problem is yet greater if the similarity assumption is inapplicable (although since firms are similarly motivated it seems probable that the similarity assumption is frequently relevant, at least in the modified form that

---

* μ is a property of the entry function, for if the prices of all inputs are parameters, the number of firms in the industry is a function of the price of the product. The equation is obtained by differentiating $C_a = m._f C_a$ by rule with respect to P_a, where C_a is total consumption (and output) of a, $_f C_a$ the consumption of output of the firm and m the number of firms in the industry; P_a is the price of the output.

member firms seek to expand activity contemporaneously). We may conclude then that such is the difficulty of applying the scale condition with any accuracy, that businessmen may be expected to rationalize it into some working rule-of-thumb. For example, cost conditions provide the firmest base from which the businessman can plan output. He may then plan to produce a definite volume of output priced at a figure to cover costs and transfer-earnings; but the price will be higher if he considers entry into the production of his own or effectively competing products to be sufficiently limited.

A premiss to the foregoing analysis is the assumption that the output obtained by the industry from a given group of inputs *does* depend upon the number of firms into which the industry is divided. If—and it has been suggested in Chapter III that this is in general more probable—the industry's output is the same irrespective of the number of firms, we cannot determine the output of the firm as has been done in this chapter. For the cost of producing a given output is the same whether it is produced by one firm or by ten, and in these circumstances the 'scale condition' gives us no assistance in determining firm's output. Rather, the level of firm's output can only be determined with reference to the firm's ability to obtain command over capital, by consideration of its historical growth, and so forth. It is interesting then to note that in these circumstances too the firm will seek to determine its level of output by a procedure which is very much the same as the 'rule-of-thumb' already suggested. A particular profit rate becomes 'normal' to an industry and the firm frequently computes its price simply on this cost-plus-profit basis and then seeks to promote sales by all means at its command. However, so long as we can unambiguously determine the output of the industry, the output of the firm is a matter of secondary interest to us in this essay and we shall not discuss it further. Henceforth we shall continue to advance the hypothesis of Chapter III that the output obtained by an industry from a given group of inputs is the same, irrespective of the number of firms into which the industry is divided.

NOTE TO CHAPTER XI

The firm's aim of maximum profit

The necessary maximum condition for the firm can be derived as follows. For brevity we shall assume that labour is the sole variable factor employed (the argument applies equally to the many-factor case). If X_a is the firm's output, n its input of labour, and P_a and P_n the prices of the output and labour respectively,

$$\text{Profit } (G) = \text{Total revenue} - \text{total cost}$$
$$= X_a \cdot P_a - n \cdot P_n.$$

Hence the rate of change of profit with respect to the input of labour (see Appendix I, p. 94),

$$\frac{dG}{dn} = \frac{d}{dn}(X_a \cdot P_a) - \frac{d}{dn}(n \cdot P_n)$$

$$= P_a \cdot \frac{dX_a}{dn} + X_a \cdot \frac{dP_a}{dn} - P_n - n \cdot \frac{dP_n}{dn}$$

$$= P_a \cdot \frac{dX_a}{dn}\left(1 + \frac{1}{\epsilon_a}\right) - P_n\left(1 + \frac{1}{\epsilon_n}\right),$$

where ϵ_a is the price elasticity of demand for a by consumers and ϵ_n is the price elasticity of demand for labour by the firm. (The price elasticity is the ratio of the percentage increase in demand to the percentage rise in price, the initiating rise in price being small.) Hence the rate of change of profit with respect to the input of labour is zero when

$$P_n = P_a \cdot \frac{dX_a}{dn} \cdot \left(\frac{1 + \dfrac{1}{\epsilon_a}}{1 + \dfrac{1}{\epsilon_n}}\right).$$

When the price of labour is fixed, ϵ_n is zero, hence we have the result

$P_n =$ the marginal revenue productivity of labour.

If the price of a is also fixed, ϵ_a is zero, hence we have the result

$P_n =$ the value of the marginal product of labour.

Example. If the firm's production function is (u, v being constants)

$$X_a = u \cdot n - v \cdot n^2,$$

we readily ascertain that (P_a, P_n being fixed) the rate of change of profit with respect to labour input is zero when
$$P_n = u - 2v \cdot n.$$

Since it is also apparent that this rate of change is diminishing (i.e. the second derivative is negative), it follows that this position of zero rate of change is also a position of maximum profit (see Appendix II, p. 98). Hence for the given levels of price of labour and output, the most profitable output is immediately computed.

Suppose there are two variable inputs n and j, then our general results read

$$P_n = P_a \cdot \frac{dX_a}{dn} \cdot \left(\frac{1 + \dfrac{1}{\epsilon_a}}{1 + \dfrac{1}{\epsilon_n}}\right),$$

and

$$P_j = P_a \cdot \frac{d \cdot X_a}{dj} \cdot \left(\frac{1 + \dfrac{1}{\epsilon_a}}{1 + \dfrac{1}{\epsilon_j}}\right).$$

Now we can rewrite these in the following form, leaving the first unchanged, but altering the second (and third and any subsequent equations for additional factors k):

$$\text{(i)} \quad P_n = P_a \cdot \frac{dX_a}{dn} \cdot \left(\frac{1 + \dfrac{1}{\epsilon_a}}{1 + \dfrac{1}{\epsilon_n}} \right),$$

and

$$\text{(ii)} \quad \frac{\dfrac{dX_a}{dn}}{P_n \left(1 + \dfrac{1}{\epsilon_a} \right)} = \frac{\dfrac{dX_a}{dj}}{P_j \left(1 + \dfrac{1}{\epsilon_j} \right)} \left[= \frac{\dfrac{dX_a}{dk}}{P_k \left(1 + \dfrac{1}{\epsilon_k} \right)} \quad \text{and so on} \right],$$

which are the necessary maximum conditions of the firm (respectively, the scale and equi-marginal productivity conditions).

If all the elasticities of demand for factors ϵ_n, ϵ_j, ϵ_k are the same (which includes the case where all factor-prices are fixed and hence $\epsilon_n = \epsilon_j = \epsilon_k = 0$) then the equi-marginal productivity condition is especially simple in form, viz. the ratio of the marginal product of a factor to its price shall be the same for all factors.

CHAPTER XII

REVIEW OF ECONOMIZING ACTIVITY

§ 1. Every economizing act by the individual either represents his solution of a problem of choice or (in the case of innovation, to be discussed later) an increase in the potential productivity of available resources. The common element, then, of the economizing activities we have examined is the existence of alternative courses of action. In each case we have asserted that the individual seeks maximum profit or satisfaction and have then ascertained which of the alternative courses will achieve this. To some extent we have been successful in identifying a calculus or automatic procedure which can immediately indicate the chosen course. The equi-marginal productivity and equi-marginal utility conditions are cases in point—determining for example the ratio of inputs or the ratio of consumer-purchases. Where the problem is not quite so simple—as in the case of location—we have none the less established a procedure for ascertaining the appropriate course of action.

Restating the position rather more formally: we have found that wherever the individual has a choice between alternative courses of action, we may record the problem as one of choosing one of a number of alternative ratios. The problem is then characteristically to ascertain first whether the ratio which maximizes the individual's position will be within certain specified positive finite limits. In many cases the solution to this may be self-evident, but if not then we must ascertain whether the ratio will be *on* a limit, for example we may know that the ratio of input of land to labour cannot exceed $\frac{1}{75}$ nor be less than $\frac{1}{100}$, but first we must check whether it will *be* $\frac{1}{75}$ or $\frac{1}{100}$; similarly if the limits are zero and infinity. If we find that the ratio is within known positive finite limits and if the ratio may vary continuously within these limits then the second phase of the problem, which is to ascertain the ratio chosen, can be solved by routine application of the infinitesimal calculus. The reader will have observed that the two parts of the problem have varied in prominence in different chapters—in discussing consumer-goods we were inclined to assume tacitly that the ratio of purchases would be positive finite, but in the analysis of location the prime problem was to ascertain precisely whether the ratio of the outputs of a commodity at two geographic points would be zero or infinity, i.e. whether production would be carried on at one location only. The general procedure is well typified by the case of choice between alternative methods of production:* it is possible that one method

---

* As already noted, production at different locations is but a special case of alternative methods of production.

76

only may be employed (i.e. the ratio of outputs of the two methods is zero or infinity) and we must follow the tedious business of testing each such possibility in turn and examining production costs in each case; if both methods will be employed the ratio of their outputs is determined by the fact that the total profit from both methods is to be maximized—the criterion which specifies the solution being in this case that, with the equi-marginal productivity condition satisfied under both methods, the prices of the product of both methods shall be the same.

§2. However, the analysis of economizing activities in this essay has left several gaps. First, we have blandly ignored the problem of exhausting resources and have assumed that factors were available for productive activity irrespective of their exhaustibility. This assumption is probably very realistic.* None the less, conservation activity is potentially of the greatest importance and our previous results are subject to this proviso. Second, while we have analysed the determination of investment in material goods, we have no way of readily treating that accumulation of personal skills which dominates modern productive systems. A closely allied deficiency has been our failure to analyse the flow of labour into alternative trades and professions—but indeed we could say little more of a general character on this score than that individuals' choice of occupation is determined by the wage as well as by the prestige, cleanliness and other attractions of each alternative† but also by existing institutions—educational opportunities, social strata, family tradition —which are frequently dominant in determining choice of occupation. Attention has also previously been drawn to our failure to do justice to the many kinds of hedging opportunities open to businessmen.

Failure to analyse fully all economizing activities is not of course the sole deficiency of the picture of the productive system drawn in the preceding chapters. For, in order to etch the structure of the productive system in bold relief, a number of simplifications have been made. To name three: the

---

* Our civilization has been little concerned at the prospect of a shrinkage of its irreplaceable resources—presumably because in a predominantly private enterprise world the date at which the shrinking would become significant has been much further off than the lifetime of an individual (who accordingly would not stand to profit himself by taking cognizance of the development). A second reason for this lack of concern has been a reliance upon continued technological change; moreover, such change involves risk for the person who proposes to buy up irreplaceable resources.

There is indeed no immediate answer, in general, to the question: How may irreplaceable resources be used most economically? For this will depend on the tastes of the person or group concerned (with particular reference to their attitude to the future), their expectations as to future wants, and their expectations as to other future changes such as technological progress. But it is impossible not to ask whether a community which ignores this problem— as it appears the present civilization has largely done—and proceeds to use up these resources as rapidly as possible, is in fact being economical—however careful it may be in making the other choices we have examined.

† Individuals seek to equalize the 'net advantages' of all occupations.

postulate that the industry's output from a given group of factors is the same irrespective of the number of firms may often only be approximately true; we have used consumption functions which represent the spending of the entire community when it might be far more interesting to stratify society according to source of income and draw up consumer-demand functions for each group or stratum; finally, we have been tacitly prepared to group the products of different firms into a single industry even though the commodities may not be wholly identical, e.g. butter factories produce branded packaged butter and so strictly speaking each factory produces a different commodity.

However, there is not one of these problems that cannot be readily analysed and absorbed into the framework of this essay. The details of productive systems are capable of infinite variation but the structure of the system is readily identified: it consists of the four kinds of institutional data originally specified and of the propensity of individuals to maximize their position wherever choice of action is available.

CHAPTER XIII

THE STATE

§1. No picture of a modern community would be complete which does not sketch, however briefly, the role of the State in determining the levels of production and price. Even in the 'capitalist' nations of the western world the State has become the most important single institution determining the level of productive activity. It is necessary therefore—without entering into excessive detail—to show how State action fits into the framework of this essay.

The State is the depository of supreme power. Apart from its—perhaps not unqualified—supremacy in the allocation of resources and hence its ability to change the results of the operations of the private sector, the State is characterized by the apparent irrelevance of any simple maximizing hypothesis and also (merely by virtue of its size) by the fact that its own expenditure significantly affects its receipts.

In so far as State activities affect production, they may be conveniently grouped under three heads:

(1) The power to tax and to spend;
(2) The power to control the banking system;
(3) The power to issue directives (*a*) changing conditions under which production is carried on (e.g. prohibitive tariff; rationalization of industry; man-power control); (*b*) specifying prices and/or quantities of goods and services to be produced or employed.

It should, however, be immediately noted that a given political objective may often be attained by measures taken under one or other of these heads—the three, though different in kind, are largely alternative.

The State can determine the basic institutions of the community in a multitude of ways it is not proposed to examine here: it can alter the distribution of ownership of resources, affect the size of the population by migration or propaganda or subsidies, seek to change tastes by advertising ('save more'; 'eat less meat'), and maintain departments devoted to industrial research. It can also affect production functions by fostering genuine infant industries. And it characteristically enforces a code of commercial and civil law, promotes education and enacts pure food regulations. These and other activities are at any time part of the institutional basis of the society and our analysis is carried on within their framework.

In order to keep the discussion within manageable bounds, only the effect on production of the power to tax and to spend will be considered here—leaving the reader to introduce the second and third powers.

§2. The two main bases on which taxation is levied are original resources and produced commodities—for instance, land tax, cigarette tax. In each case two alternative methods of levy are commonly used, namely a tax on the quantity of the resource or commodity, or on its value (i.e. quantity × price);* moreover, a levy on the basis of its value may be made either directly or by taxing its income,† these last alternatives being essentially equivalent since asset value equals the sum of discounted future incomes—for instance, taxing land either on its value or on the rent it yields.

In the case of an original resource such as land, taxation on both quantity and value is common—and value is taxed either directly or on the rental and frequently on both. As regards labour, tax on quantity is unusual (save for a poll-tax) and for fairly obvious reasons tax on value is normally levied by assessing on income. Taxes on consumption commodities are commonly in the form of sales-, expenditure-, purchase-, import- and export-taxes levied either on quantity or value (by the direct method)—and sometimes they are negative, i.e. subsidies. The same is true of non-consumption commodities but, in addition, taxation is common on the value of investment-goods by assessing on their income—this is effected by the income tax on profits-and-interest. Inheritance taxes are in essence a periodic tax (at about thirty-year intervals) on the value of original material resources *plus* a tax on the value of investment goods—although the fact that the tax is levied on the occasion of death has effects on incentive (to work, to invest) which are probably not exactly reproducible by, for example, an annual tax for thirty years on the same tax base.

§3. Taxes on commodities of everyday consumption (butter, pianos) are introduced into the overall analysis in the industry's *cost equation*:

$$\text{Value of output} = \text{the sum of factor-costs} + \text{taxation.}$$

The effect of the tax is to raise the industry's cost schedule (or supply schedule) which shows, for any given set of factor-prices and tax rates, the price the industry will charge at each possible level of output. Hence the commodity is dearer relatively to other goods; the real price of labour and of other resources is reduced; the disposable real income (i.e. nominal real income *less* tax) of consumers is reduced. The first and third counts will affect both the level and allocation of consumer-spending, and the fall in consumer-spending will also reduce the demand for investment goods and depress the interest rate; the second count may affect the supply of original resources for productive activity.‡

---

* E.g. land is sometimes taxed per acre, motor-cars usually on value at factory. Taxes are also levied on changes in value, e.g. taxes on windfalls.

† The latter alternative of course applies only where the resource or commodity has an appreciable length of life and also yields (or is at least capable of yielding) an income.

‡ This is analysed in detail below.

Taxes on investment goods (lathes, generators) similarly appear in the *cost equation* of the industry producing them. Likewise they raise the cost-schedule of any consumer-good industry using the investment good or its products. So the effects of the investment-good tax are of the same nature as those of the consumer-good tax listed in the previous paragraph. In addition, however, if there are alternative ways of producing the final consumer-good—i.e. if there is a choice whether to use the taxed investment good—then methods of production may also be affected. If, for example, there is a method of production employing less of the investment good then the tax is a stimulus to use it and so the demand for investment goods and the interest rate will be further depressed.

The above argument may be viewed from another vantage point. Suppose a 5 % sales tax were levied on the value of all consumer-goods. Then we have all the effects noted in the first paragraph of this section, save that since the relative prices of consumer-goods are unchanged there will be no price-substitution between them. If in addition to the consumer-good tax, a 2 % tax is levied on the value of all investment goods, we have a further tax on particular methods of producing consumer-goods. If any possible alternative methods of production (i.e. using fewer investment goods) are vastly less efficient, the existing methods of production will continue to be used. In such case the investment-goods tax is equivalent to a further sales tax on consumer-goods (though it would only be equivalent to a proportional sales tax if the degree of use of investment goods were the same in all consumer-good industries). Methods of production, of course, may be affected, with the further effects noted in the preceding paragraph. Finally, taxation on the investment good may be levied either by a direct tax at the time of sale or alternatively by an equivalent tax levied on the income from the investment over its working life.*

Taxes on imports into a region, i.e. tariffs, are introduced into the overall analysis in the *equi-price condition* which states that the prices of inter-regionally traded goods shall differ by their transfer-costs. The tariff is such a transfer-cost. The effects of a tariff on the imported brands of a commodity may also be achieved by an equivalent subsidy on the home-produced brands (the subsidy of course lowers the cost schedule of the home industry). In each case the home-produced substitute becomes more profitable relatively to all other home production (including production for export) and so tends to cause a transfer of resources to the protected industry.

A tax on wage-rates—the 'personal exertion income tax'—is introduced in

---

* A tax at the time of sale could be met by borrowing the amount of the tax and then repaying the loan over the working life of the equipment. The annual amount repaid on the loan (capital repayment *plus* interest) is the amount of the equivalent annual tax on the income from the investment over its working life.

the analysis in the *factor-supply function* for labour, the supply of labour being a function of the effective or disposable real wage-rate (i.e. after deduction of the tax from the nominal real wage-rate). The effects are similar in kind to those of a general sales tax on consumer-goods; the drop in disposable income reduces consumer-demand and this in turn will reduce the demand for investment goods and depress the interest rate; the fall in the effective wage-rate may affect the supply of labour.* Let us consider this latter effect in more detail. It should first be noted, however, that it has been found to be administratively simple to levy income taxes which are not proportional but progressive; e.g. instead of levying a 10 % proportional tax on income (Y) $$\text{Tax paid} = 0\cdot 1(Y),$$
a tax may be levied $$\text{Tax paid} = 0\cdot 05(Y) + 0\cdot 0001(Y)^2;$$

which is progressive in the sense that each additional £ of income raises the total tax paid by a greater amount than the previous £ of income.† Now the degree of progression of the tax formula may have an important effect on the supply of labour. For example, an individual with a £500 p.a. income will pay £50 in tax under either of the above two formulae. But the imposition of the tax affects him in two ways: a £ of his now lower income yields him more satisfaction‡ for the wants he meets are more urgent and this is a stimulus to work longer; on the other hand, from every £ of income he earns, a portion is taken in tax and this is a stimulus to work less for the effective hourly wage-rate is less. The stimulus to work less is stronger in the case of the progressive tax because out of his potential 501st £ of income the extra tax taken will be £0·1501, whereas under the proportional tax formula the extra tax is only £0·1. It is this strong disincentive effect of progressive taxation which has stopped modern 'radical' governments from using the income tax as an instrument for levelling all incomes. On the other hand, no 'reactionary'

* Even if there is a standard working week, the supply of overtime labour may be affected.

† The following table illustrates this:

Income (£)	Tax paid (£)	Increase in tax paid ('marginal tax rate')
100	6	—
101	6·0701	0·0701
102	6·1404	0·0703
103	6·2109	0·0705
104	6·2816	0·0707

This tax formula is also progressive in the less important sense that the *average* tax rate rises with income, e.g. when income is £100 p.a. the tax rate is only 6 %, but when income is £1000 p.a. the rate is 15 %.

‡ By the postulate of diminishing marginal utility.

government would attempt to rely for revenue on the poll-tax (where the marginal tax rate is zero and so the incentive to work is a maximum) for the revenue needs of modern governments are so heavy that no poll-tax could raise the required amount without reducing living standards below the level required for basic efficiency.

Taxation on land rents can be analysed in an analogous manner to the tax on wage-rates. The remaining income taxes are on interest and profits. A tax on the interest receipts from industrial debentures is equivalent to a tax on the investment goods originally financed by the debentures* and this we have already discussed. Interest receipts, of course, also come from government bonds and savings deposits and these can be readily introduced. Profits have three components apart from the pure interest return—the entrepreneurial wage, the reward for risk-bearing and a monopoly return (if any). The first of these is another form of personal exertion income and can be analysed as such, while the third can be taxed with impunity if it can be identified and separated. But the tax on the reward for risk-bearing is another matter and here again progressive taxation may have a strong disincentive effect.

§4. In discussing taxation we have clearly been looking only at one side of the penny. Just as taxation decreases aggregate demand for goods and services, so conversely does government expenditure increase aggregate demand. But government expenditure is not necessarily limited by tax receipts—funds may be obtained by borrowing from private individuals, from commercial banks or from the central bank. The three major groups of government expenditure are in general:

(1) Payment for goods and factor-services;
(2) Transfer-payments;
(3) Subsidies.

The last of these is a negative tax on commodities and so is covered by our previous discussion.

Transfer-payments are introduced into the overall analysis in the *consumer-demand functions*, for the conspicuous items among transfer-payments are pensions and other relief payments under the head of social assistance,† and their common characteristic is that they affect both the level and the distribution of the disposable national income. It is clear enough that transfer-payments raise disposable income and so consumption and hence also investment demand. In addition to this, however, the combination of progressive income tax and a social benefits scheme can leave disposable national income unchanged, yet constitutes a redistribution of the national income

* In one case the supply schedule of debentures is lifted (businessmen offer the same amount of debentures at the old price *plus* tax) and in the other case the demand schedule for debentures is depressed (owners of funds demand the same amount of debentures at the old price *less* tax). The final effect is the same.

† Some writers include interest on the national debt as a transfer-payment.

6-2

with possible major effects on both the level and allocation of consumer-spending.

State expenditure on goods and services is likewise readily introduced. State expenditure on the products of industry are introduced in the industry's *intersector condition*, which reads that in equilibrium the level of output of the industry equals the sum of its inputs into other private industries and of its given input into the State sector. State expenditure on the direct employment of original resources (land, labour) is introduced in the *factor-supply functions* as the quantity of factors available for private employment is thereby reduced. Finally, the character of the State's expenditure on goods and services is a major determinant of the use to which the community's resources are put—witness expenditure on civil administration, on armaments, on social services in kind. In whatever way this expenditure is financed, the resources purchased by State expenditure are diverted from private consumption and investment save in so far as those resources might otherwise have been unemployed.

§5. We have now shown in detail the manner in which state activities are introduced into our analysis of the determination of production. The State is introduced as 'the State sector' into which tax receipts flow and from which expenditures are made; but the important thing is to ensure that we modify

> The cost equation,
> The equi-price condition,
> The intersector condition,
> The factor-supply function,
> The consumer-demand function,

in accord with the procedure outlined above, wherever the State's revenue-expenditure measures require it.

The discussion of this chapter has been far from exhaustive—being intended to provide no more than the framework of an analysis of State activity. One omission has been State operation of business enterprises. This, however, is readily introduced into the analysis following our established procedure of introducing a privately operated industry. For example, we may have a State-owned tobacco industry which is treated in a fashion analogous to a private industry save that the State sector reaps the profits (or losses).

CHAPTER XIV

THE THEORY OF GENERAL INTERDEPENDENCE

§1. This essay has been devoted to the first elementary stage of the analysis of productive activity, namely specifying the position of equilibrium of the system. Before proceeding, it is time to admit that the seven relations set out in Chapter I, §5, are not sufficient for this purpose; in particular the three conditions (equi-marginal productivity; normal profit; intersector) are not sufficient to specify equilibrium. Three ancillary conditions* are required:

(1) That marginal revenue increases less rapidly than marginal cost for all possible factor variations;

(2) That the profit rate obtained varies inversely with the level of output of the industry;

(3) That the increase in demand for a commodity consequent upon an increment in its output is less than that increment.

There has clearly been considerable justification in the assumption, tacitly made throughout this essay, that these ancillary conditions are satisfied by the solutions to our models.

The original seven relations, together with these further three, are sufficient to specify a position† of general equilibrium with which are associated definite levels of output (and price) and from which, once obtained, no decision-making unit will seek to move. But it is only a position of possible equilibrium —nothing in this essay so far can tell us whether it will be attained. It is not enough that we know that individuals seek the equilibrium giving them maximum profits and satisfaction, for they might never hit upon that constellation of outputs and prices which no one will want to change. We must therefore address ourselves to the new problem—whether equilibrium will exist.

Let us maintain the assumptions that there is a unique possible position of equilibrium, that factors are perfectly mobile, and that decision-making units have perfect knowledge of all market transactions. Now if all units reacted instantaneously to all changes anywhere in the system and to any failure to be in equilibrium, then the possible equilibrium must exist.‡ For all conceivable combinations of values of variables may be assumed instantaneously, and

---

* They are inequalities.

† For simplicity we shall assume that there is only one possible equilibrium.

‡ Using another terminology we may paraphrase the statement 'equilibrium must exist' by saying 'the system must be stable'.

that combination corresponding to general equilibrium will accordingly be attained. Hence, on the assumptions, failure to be in equilibrium can arise only through a pattern of lagged reactions.

In order, then, to investigate the existence of equilibrium we must conceive of it in terms to which temporal analysis may be applied.* This requires that all variables are dated and all reaction times specified.† The position at which all rates of change through time are zero corresponds to what we previously called general equilibrium.

The former necessary conditions of equilibrium (equi-marginal productivity; normal profit; intersector) are accordingly replaced by relations specifying rates of change, namely: the rate of change (through time) of employment of a factor with regard to the ratio of its weighted marginal product to the weighted marginal product of the *n*th factor (the weights being the reciprocals of the respective factor-prices); the rate of change (through time) of the output of the industry with regard to the ratio of the actual profit rate to the normal profit rate; and the rate of change (through time) of industry output with regard to inventory accumulation. The ancillary (or sufficient) conditions of equilibrium are replaced by requirements covering the form of these last three relations. The general requirement is that any movement shall start towards equilibrium and in this case would be satisfied, for example, if the three relations were monotonic, and respectively direct, direct, and inverse. However, this requirement is not alone sufficient. If equilibrium is to exist, the system must not only be such that any movement starts towards equilibrium. In addition it is required that if the movement overshoots equilibrium, the system is none the less brought closer to equilibrium than before. These two sets of sufficient conditions may be called the first and second stability conditions.

In the two preceding paragraphs we have stated how a model of general interdependence may be constructed. When the institutional data describing the productive system are recorded in this form, we are able to ascertain both possible positions of equilibrium and whether they will exist. This analysis is not pursued here, since the algebra involved is not a little tedious. We shall content ourselves with the assertion that merely by glancing at the world around us (or at the columns of the financial editor) we obtain a strong presumption of stability and hence, if institutional data (including investment demand) remain invariant sufficiently long, of the existence of equilibrium or near-equilibrium states.‡

* 'The necessity of a sequence analysis is, of course, ultimately determined by the fact that the analysed variations do not occur simultaneously.' (E. Lundberg, *Studies in the Theory of Economic Expansion*, p. 46.)

† The period between the date of a rise in demand for butter and the date of the consequent adjustment in the output of butter is a reaction time.

‡ After all there is little evidence of multiple equilibria; reaction times are usually fairly

§2. To array the basic institutional data in the form of a system of general interdependence is a far more powerful mode of thought than yet appears. Consider the analysis of the preceding chapters: for a given set of institutional data we computed a possible equilibrium—let us assume it will exist; if institutional data change (say population rises or nylon is discovered) we compute a new equilibrium. This method of computing successive equilibria is useful as far as it goes, but it takes time to reach a new equilibrium and the analysis does not tell us how long or indeed precisely what is happening during the period. This deficiency is seen at its worst when we realize that if the adjustment period between equilibria is at all appreciable, a new institutional change may occur before the second equilibrium is reached, now causing the system to move to a third equilibrium position—but of course before that is reached, a third institutional change may occur....

It is seen then that a model of general interdependence permits us to analyse the movement through time of all levels of output and price—and this irrespective of whether a position of general equilibrium is ever in fact attained. The analysis of general interdependence is of course more complicated than that of general equilibrium, for the reason that the effects of an institutional change must be traced period by period through each industry affected. This procedure is a slow one, and so if the neighbourhood of equilibrium is rapidly achieved consequent upon institutional change, and if the path to equilibrium is of no intrinsic interest then our purposes may often be achieved by simply using general equilibrium analysis. However, we must beware of assuming too facilely that these conditions are satisfied and resting content with the less ambitious analysis of general equilibrium. It has, for example, been firmly suggested that when a major innovation occurs, the process of reaching equilibrium is both lengthy and tortuous. The vista which now lies before us is that of a theory of general interdependence in which the first task is to analyse the possible effects through time of the various types of institutional change. We shall conclude the essay by sketching that part of the theory which is concerned with the effects of innovation.

§3. Professor J. A. Schumpeter has advanced the view that innovation plays a quite unique role in society. His crucial idea is that, in general, when an innovation is introduced by one or more entrepreneurs the productive system as a whole does not move easily to the higher levels of production now possible. On the contrary, the innovators disrupt the productive activities of their competitors and of other firms who must adapt themselves to the new situation. Schumpeter suggests that in these successive phases of innovation

short; the first stability conditions will usually have the right signs; and the businessman is usually as careful as possible not to 'overshoot' by more than a limited margin. There are of course exceptions, e.g. if a rise in prices engenders expectation of further rise, the stability of the system may break down.

87

and adaptation, we find the essential explanation of the sequence of boom and depression characteristic of the capitalist system of production. The Schumpeterian thesis may now be stated in a little more detail.*

Schumpeter regards the capitalist system of production as a private property system distinguished by the fact that innovation is characteristically financed by bank credit. Consider then the introduction of an innovation so financed and be it observed that innovations tend to 'bunch', inasmuch as an innovation in one industry may not only be copied in that or in other industries, but also creates new opportunities in other industries. If the initiating group of innovations is large, it will be the more difficult for the rest of the system to adapt itself easily to the new situation to be described. These innovations involve new investment and (starting from near full employment) the prices of factors will be bid up and an inflationary situation develop. These rising costs create difficulties for the 'old' (i.e. non-innovating) firms which are later accentuated when the new products appear on the market to compete with the old. In addition, as the innovating firms complete their investment programme, the level of production of investment goods will fall and this will involve also a secondary fall in production in consumer-goods industries—unless it should chance that investment is simultaneously rising elsewhere in the system. Further, the innovators will proceed to repay their bank loans from current sales receipts. All these effects make it highly probable that at some stage the inflation will slacken and give place to a fall in production and prices. Other and more subtle effects may also be added to the above basic process. During the phase of rising production and prices many firms and individuals order machinery and stocks of goods on the assumption that the existing rates of increase in demand for their products will continue. The mere slackening of these rates of increase will cause inventory liquidation and reduction in investment-demand.

It is not intended here to enter into a full discussion of business fluctuations. Clearly the depression, once developed, will not continue indefinitely, if only because of the ultimate revival in replacement investment. It is sufficient to have indicated that innovation, although the ultimate economizing activity through which a higher real income is possible, may move the system along a difficult path before the new equilibrium is reached.

* See J. A. Schumpeter, *Business Cycles*.

A NOTE ON
NON-HOMOGENEITY OF PRODUCT

In developing the theoretical system it has been assumed in the text that the output of an industry is homogeneous. This implies two assumptions: first, that the production of one commodity places no constraint on the firm as to the production of any other commodity, i.e. the production of different commodities is technically independent; second, that the members of an industry do in fact produce but one commodity (technical independence being only a necessary condition for this to prevail). The problems to be faced under each of these two heads will now be surveyed in turn.

In considering whether the production of different commodities is technically independent, attention may first be drawn to one sense in which dependence may be quite normal: the firm may seek to hedge by diversifying its output and this may even lead to the choice of less specific methods of production. However, because of almost complete lack of data on this matter, we shall proceed on the assumption that any hedging which occurs does not affect methods of production. Hedging apart, then, technical dependence between the production of different commodities may be complete or partial. The former is the case where the commodities must be produced in fixed proportions. The latter is that in which there is choice of what this proportion shall be. (This opportunity for choice may be properly regarded as an extension of the fifth opportunity for economizing activity, viz. the choice as to the ratio between inputs.)

In the case of fixed proportions, the form of the production function offers no difficulty—the several commodities form a 'composite product'. In the variable proportions case, possible forms of the (joint) production function are suggested by the transformation curve joining all possible output-combinations. For example, in a simple case of two outputs (x, y) and a single input, the transformation curve might take one of the forms in Fig. 13 (the input (w) being constant), having equations (within the bounds) of the following form

$$x = a - by, \quad x = a - by^2, \quad (x-a).(y-b)^m = c.$$

Now the output of x depends, first, upon the scale of activity (i.e. the level of input of w) and, secondly, the output of y relatively to the input of w. By building these two characteristics into the equations of the transformation curves we obtain production functions of the following form:

$$x = \left(a - b.\frac{y}{w}\right).w^t, \quad x = \left[a - b.\left(\frac{y}{w}\right)^2\right].w^t, \quad x = \left[a + \frac{c}{\left(\frac{y}{w} - b\right)^m}\right].w^t.$$

89

If returns to scale are of unit elasticity ($t=1$), we have

$$x = aw - by, \quad x = aw - b\frac{y^2}{w}, \quad x = aw + \frac{cw}{\left(\frac{y}{w} - b\right)^m},$$

respectively.

If the third case is that of a rectangular hyperbolic transformation curve ($m=1$), then we have $x = aw + \dfrac{cw^2}{y - bw}$. However, what the characteristic forms may be in practice is a matter for detailed practical investigation.

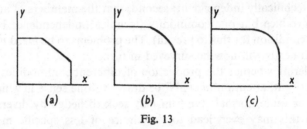

Fig. 13

There are in general determinate levels of output under joint production, the system of equations describing the industry being only slightly more complicated than under simple production. The important new point is that the equi-marginal productivity condition is extended such that if the two commodities i and j are being jointly produced, then the ratio of the marginal productivity of j to its price equals the ratio of the marginal productivity (in producing i) of the nth factor to its price.* The marginal product of j is the increase in the production of i which results (all inputs being unchanged) from a fall in production of j by one unit. This extension of the equi-marginal productivity condition determines the ratio in which i and j will be produced. For the rest, there are as many intersector conditions as goods produced and of course wherever the value of output of the industry appears (as in the cost equation and normal profit condition), this is the sum of the values of the individual outputs. The analysis in the text can then be promptly extended to handle joint production.

Let us turn now to the second assumption. Even if the production of commodities is not technically dependent, a firm may produce a number of commodities. The reason for this may lie merely in custom, but is more likely to lie in the fact that production of commodities which are in some sense 'similar' or 'related' is either expected by customers or is an obvious method

---

* More generally we must allow for the fact that price is a variable and hence the marginal productivity of j is weighted, not simply by the reciprocal of its price P_j, but by the reciprocal of $P_j\left(1 + \dfrac{1}{e_j}\right)$ where e_j is the elasticity of demand for j.

of expanding the volume of the firm's output. As previously pointed out, where the firm carries on a number of distinct and separable activities it is probably best to separate these out and risk the ensuing problems of imputation. However, there are two other possibilities open to us which may sometimes be convenient.

Where the several products differ only in size or shape and where in consequence not only do the several products absorb the same inputs in the same proportions but also the rate of transformation between two products is a constant, then we may reduce all products to their 'equivalent' in terms of some one product.

There is always the remaining possibility that if the several products are produced in fixed proportions we can regard them as a 'composite product' and proceed straightforwardly. However, this possibility is an unlikely one and while failure to satisfy the assumption might be met by 'weighting' the several commodities, the meaning of such a procedure is rather dubious if the products are not of the same character.

We conclude that where several goods are produced, although not jointly, the two reliable procedures are either to separate out activities or (in a limited range of cases) to reduce to a common equivalent.

A NOTE ON MONOPOLY

This note elaborates the writer's approach to monopoly more fully than seemed necessary in the text.

There are two sources of monopoly power to be distinguished. Consider first the case where all firms in an industry are producing the same commodity. Competition is that circumstance in which firms are free to enter indefinitely into the production of the industry's homogeneous commodity. Monopoly is that circumstance in which, because entry is restricted by some means, firms are able to adopt policies establishing a dual-price for entrepreneurship (i.e. a higher entrepreneurial wage within the industry than without).* Such policies may be termed 'tactical' or 'oligopolistic' but are not analysed here and the monopoly control over supply which they establish is recorded in the entry function, e.g. a higher 'normal profit' in this industry than in others. Consequently monopolistic positions in the various industries may be ascertained by examination of the relative normal profit rates which they succeed in obtaining† —so long as these are net of risk payment and non-profit elements.‡ This incidentally brings out the fundamentally *relative* character of the monopoly concept. Restriction by one monopolistic group of firms means in general that factors are reallocated from that to other industries (unless a reduction in aggregate demand is created). Nor can the degree of monopoly be stated in absolute terms unless some one industry is known to receive only transfer-costs.

A firm may also seek to increase its share of the industry's sales by 'differentiating' its product, e.g. by branding its article and by advertising the brand. Though differentiation is most conveniently regarded as a process by which the industry's total sales are reallocated between the member firms, it does potentially offer the individual firm a monopoly power analogous to that previously examined. (Where before the industry was sole producer of its product, so here the firm is sole producer of its differentiated product.) However in this essay, differentiation of the product within the industry is ignored. We are not intrinsically interested in the reallocation of sales between member firms and if, as I suggest, differentiation has no other major effects§ then the practical application of the analysis becomes greatly simplified.

* This dual-price definition may be generalized to apply to monopolistic action on the part of the custodians of any original factor.

† For simplicity we may assume that no industry can affect the prices of its factors.

‡ In practice, observed 'profit' must be adjusted for variations in risk and entrepreneurial ability, and for imputed returns to natural advantages such as location, shallow mines, non-militant labour.

§ This is not to deny that industry consumer-demand curves are impervious to the blandishments of advertising, nor that advertising costs are a significant portion of national expenditure. These elements can be readily introduced.

After this excursus into the meaning of monopoly power, the reason for the failure to analyse its formation in the present essay may be made clearer by analogy. In the treatment of consumer-demand we exclude the concept of utility (and of preference) from the system of relations because, however interesting, it is superfluous to the analysis of the productive system in operational terms. The concept of monopoly (and of competition) is similarly superfluous. In sum, we do not deny the importance of the question as to how an entry function (or factor supply function) comes to have a particular form —any more than we deny the importance of the same question in the case of the consumer-demand function. Our present method is wholly determined by the fact that we can in practice ascertain the foregoing functions (or something very like them) in quantitative terms and can then apply the system of relations. However, if one of these functions is replaced by a number of 'more fundamental' relations determining it, then we find that the system of relations can no longer be empirically ascertained.

APPENDIX I

THE MEANING OF MARGINAL PRODUCTIVITY AND OF OTHER MARGINAL CONCEPTS

§1. The purpose of this discussion is to explain briefly the meaning of the 'marginal' concept and to show how its numerical value may be found. The 'marginal productivity' of a factor employed by a firm is the *rate* at which the firm's output changes in relation to the input of the factor. We wish to ascertain this rate.

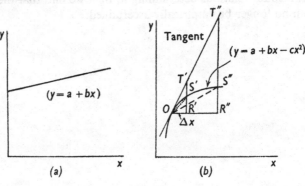

Fig 14

§2. We begin with the concept of a continuous function (or functional relation) of which two examples are illustrated (Fig. 14). Such a functional relation expresses the fact that, knowing the value of x, the value of y is also known (a, b and c being constants). We may state this more briefly by simply writing

$$y = f(x) \quad \text{or} \quad y = \phi(x).^*$$

We wish to know the rate at which y changes in relation to x—and this rate has, for any particular value of x, a graphical representation as the slope of the tangent to the curve in Fig. 14 (*b*).

Suppose that, for the second-degree function, the independent variable increases from the value of x to the value $(x + \Delta x)$. Associated with this is

---

* The symbols read: 'y is a function of x'. For example, if

$$y = a + bx - cx^2$$

were (over the range of x indicated) the production function of a coal mine where x represents man-hours of labour and y is tons of coal, then a knowledge of x gives a knowledge of y. Coal output rises with the increase in man-hours worked, but at a decreasing rate.

94

a movement of the dependent variable from the value y to that of $(y+\Delta y)$. The corresponding *average* rate of change of y per unit increase of x is $\Delta y/\Delta x$; and as

$$\Delta y = (y+\Delta y)-y \qquad \text{... (difference)}$$
$$= a+b(x+\Delta x)-c(x+\Delta x)^2-(a+bx-cx^2) \quad \text{... (substitute)}$$
$$= b.\Delta x-2c.x.\Delta x-c.(\Delta x)^2 \qquad \text{... (simplify)}$$
$$\frac{\Delta y}{\Delta x} = b-2c.x-c.\Delta x. \qquad \text{... (divide)}$$

Hence the

$$\text{Limit of } \frac{\Delta y}{\Delta x} = b-2c.x. \qquad \text{... (limit)}$$

as $\Delta x \to 0$.

So we find, as indeed is clear from Fig. 14 (*b*), that the average rate of change in y per unit increase in x has a definite limiting value as the change in x approaches zero, i.e. as $OR(\Delta x)$ becomes smaller, $RS(\Delta y)$ becomes more nearly equal to RT and so RS/OR (or $\Delta y/\Delta x$) becomes more nearly equal to RT/OR (the slope of the tangent).* This limiting value is the slope at the point of tangency and is the rate which we sought.† A shorthand expression for this limiting value is dy/dx, called the derivative or *differential coefficient* of the dependent variable y with respect to x. (Note that this derivative is not a ratio, nor is it equal to $\Delta y/\Delta x$, but it is approximately equal to this last ratio when Δx approximates to zero.)

By applying precisely the steps of the above argument to the general case of any power function $y=x^n$ (n being any power), we can not only show that $dy/dx=n.x^{n-1}$, but can also frame rules for the derivation (i.e. obtaining the limiting rates of change) of combination of functions.‡ Some more important results so obtained are:

where

$$z=\phi(x), \ w=\mu(x), \text{ and } t=f(x)$$

I.
$$\frac{d}{dx}(z+w-t)=\frac{dz}{dx}+\frac{dw}{dx}-\frac{dt}{dx}.$$

II.
$$\frac{d}{dx}(z.w)=w.\frac{dz}{dx}+z.\frac{dw}{dx}.$$

III.
$$\frac{d}{dx}\left(\frac{z}{w}\right)=\frac{w.\frac{dz}{dx}-z.\frac{dw}{dx}}{w^2}.$$

* In fig. 14(*b*) the slope of the dotted line approaches that of the tangent much more nearly than the slope of the broken line, for the change in x is smaller.

† Thus in the example of the coal mine we have the result that the marginal productivity of labour is $(b-2c.x)$.

‡ Suppose we wished to ascertain the rate of change of the coal mine's profit with regard to the input of labour. Profit equals total revenue less total cost and each of these is a function of the input of labour. Hence to obtain our answer we require Rule I: the derivative of a sum or difference is the sum or difference of the respective derivatives (see p. 74).

Finally where, as in the above example, the derivative

$$\frac{dy}{dx}=b-2c.x$$

bears a functional relation to the independent variable, *successive differentiation* is possible.* By repeating the above method we find that the second derivative

$$\frac{d^2y}{dx^2}\left(\text{i.e.,}\ \frac{d}{dx}.\left(\frac{dy}{dx}\right)\right)=-2c.$$

§ 3. It has been stated above that the limit, when $\Delta x \to 0$, of $\Delta y/\Delta x$ is customarily a definite quantity denoted by $\frac{dy}{dx}$.

Hence it follows that in such cases

$$\frac{\Delta y}{\Delta x}=\frac{dy}{dx}+\epsilon,\ \text{where}\ \epsilon \to 0\ \text{as}\ \Delta x \to 0;$$

i.e.
$$\Delta y=\frac{dy}{dx}.\Delta x+\epsilon.\Delta x.$$

Therefore, if Δx be very small, it follows that

$$\Delta y=\frac{dy}{dx}.\Delta x \text{ approximately,} \qquad (1)$$

and the smaller is Δx the more nearly does this become true since ϵ becomes less and less with Δx. (I.e. the term $(\epsilon.\Delta x)$ becomes smaller and smaller in comparison with the other two terms, or as it is usually expressed, $\epsilon.\Delta x$ is a small quantity of higher order than Δx or Δy.)

Hence, if we choose a unit of measurement of x which is sufficiently small, then for a unit increase in x there is an increase in y which is measured by dy/dx. (The expression on the right-hand side of equation (1) is called the *differential* of y.)

Example. If we are considering a production function for the product y, then dy/dx is the *marginal productivity* of the factor x, whilst Δy is the *marginal product* of x. Under the conditions just stated, the former provides a measure of the latter.

§ 4. The foregoing argument may be applied generally to power functions. For example, $y=a+bx-cx^2$ may be, not a production function, but a simple type of consumption function where x is the individual's income and y is the quantity of commodity (or group of commodities) he chooses to purchase. In this case dy/dx is his 'marginal propensity to consume'. Or again, the 'marginal utility' of a commodity y is the addition to the total utility or satisfaction the individual obtains from his consumption of the commodity when his rate of consumption increases by a given (small) unit.

Finally, we may wish to measure the *elasticity* of the dependent variable

* This gives us the rate of change of marginal productivity.

relatively to the independent variable, i.e. an index of the responsiveness of y which is independent of the particular units in which x and y are measured. Such an index is

$$\frac{\Delta y \div y}{\Delta x \div x},$$

which gives us the ratio of the percentage change in y to the corresponding percentage change in x. So long as the increment in x is small, we know that this elasticity is approximately measured by

$$\frac{dy}{dx} \cdot \frac{x}{y}.$$

Example. In the last illustration of a consumption function, this expression measures the elasticity of the individual's demand for the commodity y in response to a change in his income.

§5. The above analysis of the process of derivation (i.e. ascertaining rates of change) is applicable without modification to power functions of two or more variables.

In the continuous function*

$$y = a \cdot x^h \cdot z^j \quad (a, h, j \text{ being constants})$$

y is a function of two independent variables x and z—these being neither dependent on one another nor both functions of another independent variable.

To obtain the partial derivative ($\partial y/\partial x$) of y with respect to x, z remaining unchanged at a given value, we proceed with the derivation as before:

$$\partial y/\partial x = a \cdot h \cdot x^{h-1} \cdot z^j.$$

Successive differentiation is likewise carried out as before:

$$\frac{\partial^2 y}{\partial x^2} = a \cdot h \cdot (h-1) \cdot x^{h-2} \cdot z^j,$$

and we may also ascertain the cross partial derivative

$$\frac{\partial^2 y}{\partial x \cdot \partial z} \left(= \frac{\partial}{\partial z} \cdot \frac{\partial y}{\partial x} \right) = a \cdot h \cdot j \cdot x^{h-1} \cdot z^{j-1}.$$

Example. If x and z are respectively the inputs of land and labour producing (say, wheat) then $\frac{\partial y}{\partial x}$ is the marginal productivity of land, $\frac{\partial^2 y}{\partial x^2}$ the rate at which that marginal productivity changes with the input of land, and $\frac{\partial^2 y}{\partial x \cdot \partial z}$ the rate at which the marginal productivity of land changes as the input of labour is changed.

* This is a form of the production function used in Chapter III.

APPENDIX II

THE MAXIMUM PROBLEM

The aim of the following is to set out briefly the method by which a maximum problem may be solved, e.g. that of the entrepreneur seeking to decide what levels of output (and input) will maximize his profit. We may restate the problem in the terms used in Appendix I:

We wish to ascertain the value of x for which the dependent variable y is a maximum, in the case where $y=f(x)$ is a continuous power function.

Geometrically (see Fig. 15), the first derivative $f'(x)$ $(=dy/dx$, the slope of the tangent) at a point is the slope of the curve. If $f'(x)$ is positive at a point the curve is rising, if it is zero the height of the curve is stationary, if negative the curve is falling as x increases.

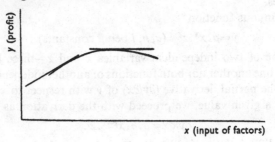

Fig. 15

Geometrically, the second derivative $f''(x)$ $(=d^2y/dx^2$, the rate of change of $dy/dx)$ gives the rate of change of slope of the curve. In everyday language, if $f''(x)$ is positive at a point, the curve is convex to the x axis; if negative, concave to the x axis; and if zero, there is neither convexity nor concavity.*

This leads to the following criteria for maximum (and minimum) values:

(1) All maximum and minimum values of $f(x)$ occur where $f'(x)=0$.

(2) If $f'(a)=0$ and $f''(a)<0$, then $f(a)$ is a maximum value of the function;†
    if $f'(a)=0$ and $f''(a)>0$, then $f(a)$ is a minimum value of the function.

Example. A simple example is given on p. 74. Entrepreneur's profit, which is to be maximized, equals the difference between total revenue and total cost—each of which are in turn a function of the input of labour. Profit is accordingly differentiated with respect to labour and the level of input at which the first derivative is zero (the second derivative being negative) is a position of maximum profit.

* We need not consider this third possibility here. An inflexional value of the function $f(x)$ can only occur at a point where $f''(x)=0$.
† I.e. x having the value a.

SELECT BIBLIOGRAPHY

AMERICAN ECONOMIC ASSOCIATION. *Readings in Business Cycle Theory* (Philadelphia: Blakiston, 1944).

ANDREWS, P. W. S. *Manufacturing Business* (London: Macmillan, 1949).

ANGELL, J. W. *The Behavior of Money* (New York: McGraw Hill, 1936).

BOWLEY, A. L. *The Mathematical Groundwork of Economics* (Oxford, 1924).

BRETHERTON, R. F., BURCHARDT, F. A. and RUTHERFORD, R. S. G. *Public Investment and the Trade Cycle in Great Britain* (Oxford, 1941).

CARLSON, S. *A Study on the Pure Theory of Production* (London: King, 1939).

CAUNT, G. W. *Introduction to the Infinitesimal Calculus* (Oxford, 1924).

HABERLER, G. *The Theory of International Trade* (London: Hodge, 1936).

HICKS, J. R. *Value and Capital*, 2nd ed. (Oxford, 1948).

INTERNATIONAL LABOUR OFFICE. *Public Investment and Full Employment*, N.S. 3 (Montreal, 1946).

KALDOR, N. Appendix C to W. Beveridge, *Full Employment in a Free Society* (London: Allen and Unwin, 1944).

KEYNES, J. M. *The General Theory of Employment, Interest and Money* (London: Macmillan, 1936).

LEAGUE OF NATIONS. *International Currency Experience*, II, A, 4 (1944).

LEONTIEF, W. *The Structure of American Economy, 1919–1939* (New York, Oxford, 1951).

LUNDBERG, E. *Studies in the Theory of Economic Expansion* (London: King, 1937).

MACHLUP, F. *International Trade and the National Income Multiplier* (Philadelphia: Blakiston, 1943).

MARSHALL, A. *Principles of Economics*, 8th ed. (London: Macmillan, 1927).

OHLIN, B. *Interregional and International Trade* (Harvard University Press, 1935).

OSGOOD, W. F. and GRAUSTEIN, W. C. *Plane and Solid Analytic Geometry* (New York: Macmillan, 1921).

PHELPS BROWN, E. H. *The Framework of the Pricing System* (London: Chapman and Hall, 1936).

REDDAWAY, W. B. *The Economics of a Declining Population* (London: Allen and Unwin, 1939).

SELECT BIBLIOGRAPHY

SAYERS, R. S. *Modern Banking*, 3rd ed. (Oxford, 1951).

SCHULTZ, H. *Theory and Measurement of Demand* (University of Chicago Press, 1938).

SCHUMPETER, J. A. *Business Cycles* (2 vols.) (New York: McGraw Hill, 1939).

STIGLER, G. J. *The Theory of Price* (New York: Macmillan, 1946).

STONE, J. R. N. and JACKSON, E. F. 'Economic Models with Special Reference to Mr Kaldor's System.' *Economic Journal*, 1946.

STONE, J. R. N. 'The Analysis of Market Demand.' *Journal of the Royal Statistical Society*, 1945.

TRIFFIN, R. *Monopolistic Competition and General Equilibrium Theory* (Harvard University Press, 1940).

100

INDEX

Printed in the United States
By Bookmasters